"BUT EVEN THOUGH WE,
OR AN ANGEL FROM HEAVEN,
SHOULD PREACH TO YOU A GOSPEL
CONTRARY TO THAT WHICH
WE HAVE PREACHED TO YOU,
LET HIM BE ACCURSED"
(GAL. 1:8).

---

*Paul of Tarsus*

# THE EDGE OF DEATH

## Phillip J. Swihart

INTER-VARSITY PRESS
DOWNERS GROVE
ILLINOIS 60515

InterVarsity Press is the book publishing division of Inter-Varsity Christian Fellowship, a student movement active on campus at hundreds of universities, colleges and schools of nursing. For information about local and regional activities, write IVCF, 233 Langdon St., Madison, WI 53703.

All Scripture quotations, unless otherwise indicated, are from the New American Standard Bible, © The Lockman Foundation 1960, 1962, 1963, 1968, 1971, 1972, 1973, 1975, and are used by permission.

Quotations from Life after Life by Raymond A. Moody, Jr., M.D., are copyright © 1975 by Raymond A. Moody, Jr. A Bantam/Mockingbird Book. Reprinted by permission of Bantam Books, Inc. and Mockingbird Books.

Quotations from Reflections on Life after Life by Raymond A. Moody, Jr., M.D. are copright © 1977 by Raymond A. Moody, Jr. A Bantam/ Mockingbird Book, Reprinted by permission of Bantam Books, Inc. and Mockingbird Books.

Quotations from "The Miracle of Kübler-Ross" by Ann Nietzke in Human Behavior (September 1977) are © 1977 Human Behavior. Reprinted by permission.

Excerpts from Journeys Out of the Body by Robert A. Monroe are copyright © 1971 by Robert A. Monroe. Used by permission of Doubleday & Company, Inc.

Distributed in Canada through InterVarsity Press, 1875 Leslie St., Unit 10, Don Mills, Ontario M3B 2M5, Canada.

ISBN 0-87784-364-3
Library of Congress Catalog Card Number:

Printed in the United States of America

## Acknowledgments

I would like to thank Dr. James W. Sire of InterVarsity Press for his special contribution to this book. Dr. Sire invested many hours in his efforts to assist me in the development of the manuscript—far beyond the contribution expected of editors—and his imprint and influence are clearly evident throughout. In a sense, Dr. Sire is a co-author and I am indebted to him.

I also appreciate the review comments of Russell Sorensen and of Judson Swihart.

Two individuals who graciously permitted very personal experiences to be shared within these pages, Anne Schweickart and Jerry Walker, deserve special recognition and I am grateful for their contributions.

# The Inviting Darkness: Introduction

# 1

Anne, my mother-in-law, recovered from a close brush with death with a very mysterious and intriguing experience to relate. She had required surgery to correct a problem within her pituitary gland which lies under the frontal lobe of the brain. Immediately following the operation she became far too lethargic, and her neurosurgeon became concerned that she might not survive.

During this critical time, she later reported that she was "conscious" of seeing her field of vision divided in half. On the one side was a soft darkness and on the other side an agitated blackness. Dividing them was a brilliant light that looked like a center-line of an asphalt highway. She knew that the blackness was life and the soft darkness death. The soft

**10**

darkness, she found, was extremely warm and inviting; at first it accepted her. Left to her own desires, she wished very much to drift on into the dark until it completely enveloped her. She felt no desire to return to normal life; she can remember no concerns for her family nor sadness in leaving them behind. Rather, she said, she was totally immersed in the "most holy" experience of her life.

At this point, however, something or some force within the soft darkness would not allow her to continue further in this direction and, in effect, forced her to move back across the line into that which represented life. After a period of intensive care, she regained consciousness—as we normally think of consciousness.

**A Challenge to Christian Understanding**  As a Christian who believes that the Bible speaks truth in all that it affirms, I began to wrestle with the question of how such an experience could fit with biblical teachings. One thing I discovered in the months since Anne recovered was that a number of individuals have written or told about similar near-death experiences. These anecdotes have come from a diverse sample of people who for a short time were considered to be clinically dead, that is, dead in terms of common medical criteria. I have also become aware of those who claim to have experienced a release from the physical body into a spirit state although they were not dying at the time.

The discovery of many common elements in these reported experiences has led some of those investigating these phenomena to some rather startling conclusions. If correct, these conclusions would have very disturbing implications for the major doctrines of the Christian faith as it has been historically understood and would certainly challenge belief in the infallibility of the Bible upon which these doctrines stand or fall.

Christians, therefore, need to examine these edge-of-death accounts and reports of out-of-the-body experiences. And we also need to analyze the conclusions and interpretations that have been drawn from these experiences by other investigators.

**Unhand Me, Gray-beard Loon!**   From the outset we should realize that our investigations will lead us into some very strange material. Much of our discussion will border on matters which are considered occult, and we may not be used to hearing such things as we are about to hear. C. Stephen Board, editor of *Eternity* magazine, has commented, "Anyone who has ever wandered into an occult bookstore knows this sensation, for their books ... are filled with strange and exotic reports that would require a lifetime to check and confirm."[1] One feels, Board says, like the man who shouted at the ancient mariner in Coleridge's poem: "Hold off! Unhand me, gray-beard loon!" The experiences we are going to examine may well leave us confused and dizzy.

Moreover, you as a reader will undoubtedly find yourself asking more questions about the material you are reading than you are finding answers for. I have found it extremely difficult to organize the book and thus certainly appreciate the frustration that you may find in following my argument without having all of your questions answered at once. Reading this book may be like rabbit hunting in a field filled with rabbits. As you walk through the brush, more rabbits are scared up than you can possibly bag. May I ask you then to hold your questions in abeyance in the hope that I will indeed consider them in due time.

A tremendous amount of material is available on the afterlife. To bring order out of this chaos, I have chosen to focus my account on only three of the major students of the subject: Dr. Raymond A. Moody, Jr., Dr. Elisabeth Kübler-Ross and Mr. Robert A. Monroe. Readers who wish to investigate the topic further may wish to consult the selective annotated bibliography at the end of the book.

In any case, my plan is first to summarize the investigations and findings of Moody, Kübler-Ross and Monroe in the next three chapters and then in the final two chapters to examine in some detail the implications of these findings in light of the biblical teaching on life after death.

# The Near-Death Experience: Raymond A. Moody, Jr.

# 2

Dr. Raymond A. Moody, Jr., the author of *Life after Life* and its sequel, *Reflections on Life after Life*, holds a Ph.D. in philosophy from the University of Virginia. He taught in this field for a number of years before making a decision to attend medical school and become a psychiatrist. In the course of his academic and professional pursuits, Dr. Moody became interested in the phenomenon of death and specifically in accounts of near-death experiences. In *Life after Life*, Moody mentions that he has found at least 150 such cases which fall into three categories:

(1) The experiences of persons who were resuscitated after having been thought, adjudged, or pronounced clinically dead by their doctors.

(2) The experiences of persons who, in the course

of accidents or severe injury or illness, came very close to physical death.

(3) The experiences of persons who, as they died, told them to other people who were present. Later, these other people reported the content of the death experience to me.[1]

**Fifteen Characteristics and More**     From these reports, Moody discovered fifteen common qualities, although no one person's account contains all such components. And, he admits, many individuals recall nothing at all during such a crisis, and several have found it almost impossible to put what they experienced into words. This leads us to the first element Moody lists as common to near-death experiences.

1. *Ineffability*. Ineffability refers to the difficulty in communicating in language what was experienced. Many who were able to verbalize in some fashion what they encountered tell what are to me utterly fascinating and wondrous stories that excite my sense of curiosity while leaving me somewhat puzzled.[2]

2. *Hearing the News*. Some individuals report that they recall hearing themselves pronounced dead by medical personnel or others present, and these reports correspond closely to what observers recall was said at that time. The fact that the sense of hearing often is the last sense modality to be lost and that people often remember what was said although apparently unconscious or under general anesthesia has been previously well documented.[3]

3. *Peace and Quiet*. Many individuals experienced very pleasant feelings of peace, quiet and

"extreme comfort" during this time.

4. *Noise.* One sensation that some found unpleasant which occurred at or near death was a distinct noise described variously as a buzzing, roaring, ringing or whistling sound. Others reported hearing beautiful music.

5. *Tunnel.* The sensation of moving very quickly through a dark space, tunnel, cave or void, often accompanied by the noise, is fairly common. One individual explained that he felt as though he were "moving in a vacuum, just through blackness. . . . It was like being in a cylinder which had no air in it. It was a feeling of limbo, of being half-way here, and half-way somewhere else."[4]

6. *Out-of-the-Body Experience.* After moving rapidly through this black void or tunnel, individuals are often amazed to find themselves suddenly viewing their own body from some point outside of it. One woman recalled looking at a scene in her hospital room in which a nurse was attempting to give her mouth-to-mouth resuscitation; the woman's out-of-the-body vantage point was from behind her own head.

This out-of-the-body experience (OOBE) varied from individual to individual. Some had no feelings toward their physical body after leaving it. Others felt sorry to see their body mangled or damaged. A few people reported that after sensing release from their bodies they no longer felt that they had any body at all but rather that "they were 'pure' consciousness,"[5] which Moody refers to as their "spiritual body."[6]

Individuals in their spiritual body but out of their physical body often reported feeling frustrated because they wanted to communicate with others in the room. However, physicians, nurses and others working around that person's body sometimes looked straight toward where that person perceived himself to be, but they gave no sign that they ever saw him or her. Those who were out of the body felt that they were floating in space, invisible, suspended in time, without the ability to communicate verbally with others.

7. *Meeting Others.* Some individuals indicated a feeling of loneliness, but that feeling was dispelled when others—deceased relatives or friends—came to aid them during this transitional period.[7] Occasionally these others told the individual that it was not yet their time to die and so they must "return to their physical bodies."[8]

8. *The Being of Light.* The common component which Moody indicates "has the most profound effect upon the individual is the encounter with a very bright light." This "being of light" is a "personal being" with "a very definite personality." Moreover, "the love and the warmth which emanate from this being to the dying person are utterly beyond words, and he feels completely surrounded by it and taken up in it, completely at ease and accepted in the presence of this being. He senses an irresistible magnetic attraction to this light."[9]

The identification of the being of light by those encountering it appears to vary as a function of the religious background and beliefs of each individual. Most of those who identify themselves as Christians decide that the being is Christ. One woman thought of the Scripture which quotes Jesus as saying, "I am the light of the world." Some of those who are Jewish believe the light to be an angel while others attach no particular label to this personality.

Communication with the being of light is reported to be a matter of thought transfer, as is communication with other spirits, rather than in the form of overt verbal language. Thus there is said to be "no possibility whatsoever either of misunderstanding or of lying to the light."[10]

The person is usually given a thought from the being of light: "Are you prepared to die? ... What have you done with your life that is sufficient?"[11] One type of question stresses preparation while the other stresses accomplishment. The questions are felt to involve no condemnation whatsoever.

9. *Life in Review.* Following these initial questions, many individuals were presented with an almost instantaneous vivid review of their entire life. It is described as somewhat like very rapid memory in which two things are stressed: "learning to love other people and acquiring knowledge."[12]

10. *The Border.* In a few of the reported near-death experiences, the individuals felt that they approached a border or limit. After moving through a dark passage, one person saw a beautiful, polished door, with no knob. He says, "I looked up and said, 'Lord, here I am. If you want me, take me.' Boy, he shot me back so fast it felt like I almost lost my breath."[13]

11. *Return.* Obviously, none of the individuals involved in Moody's research were, in fact, dead in the usual sense of that word, at least until after they had reported their experiences. Many of them reported, as did my mother-in-law, no desire to return to their physical bodies. Some felt that they still had unfin-

ished tasks to complete and thus were happy to be back. Others thought that they were "*allowed* to live by 'God,' or by the being of light."[14] Others thought that "the love or prayers of others have in effect pulled them back from death regardless of their own wishes."[15]

12. *Reporting the Experience.* Many who have experienced such an approach to death are reluctant to talk about it. They fear that others will not understand and will consider them to be emotionally unstable or the victim of an hallucinatory episode. Thus many have remained silent about what happened to them.

13. *Changed Lives.* Near-death experiences often cause people to become "more reflective and more concerned with ultimate philosophical issues."[16] A few report the acquisition of abilities which might be called psychic. Many of these individuals feel that now their mission in life is to learn to love others in a profound manner, and they have a new sense of the importance of seeking knowledge. Moody states, "Their vision left them with new goals, new moral principles, and a renewed determination to try to live in accordance with them, but with no feelings of instantaneous salvation or of moral infallibility."[17]

14. *New View of Death.* A very important and common result of such an encounter with death and with the being of light has been a change in views and beliefs about death. Most indicate that they no longer fear death. One man who had suffered from such fears since childhood said, "I believe that the Lord may have sent this experience to me because of the way I felt about death. Of course, my parents comforted me, but the Lord *showed* me, whereas they

couldn't do that."[18] However, many other patients not identifying themselves as Christians also lost their fear of death.

Moody reports that even those who formerly held "traditional" views of life after death moved away from that view after their experience. No one, he says, described a heaven or a hell. In fact, "in most cases, the reward-punishment model of the afterlife is abandoned and disavowed, even by many who had been accustomed to thinking in those terms."[19]

In the sequel to his initial investigation, however, Moody reports that a few individuals have since reported "catching glimpses of other realms of being which might well be termed 'heavenly.' "[20] Some individuals describe "a city of light" or a place of perfect peace which they feel may correspond to descriptions of heaven found in the Bible. In the examples Moody offers, however, none of the individuals encountered God or Jesus in this "heaven."

Moody also tempers his previous statements about the nonexistence of a literal hell. "It remains true," he says, "that in the mass of material I have collected no one has ever described to me a state like the archetypical hell. However, . . . I have never interviewed anyone who had been a real rounder prior to his close call. The people I have interviewed have been normal, nice people. Such transgressions as they were guilty of had been minor—the sorts of things we have all done. So one would not expect that they would have been consigned to a fiery pit. Yet nothing I have encountered precludes the possibility of a hell."[21] He further says, "There may well be a Final Judgment; near-death experiences in no way imply the contrary." And he points out that many people he has interviewed indeed still believe in it, though "they accept this on the basis of scriptural authority alone and did not derive it from anything they learned or foresaw while in their state of near or apparent 'death.' "[22] Moody adds, in concert with his first book, that "the judgment in the cases I studied came not from the being of light . . . but rather from within the individual being judged."[23]

15. *Corroboration.* The final common element in Moody's sample of near-death reports is the fact that many of them can be independently corroborated by witnesses who were known to be present or can be confirmed by other events. Moody reports that a number of physicians were amazed when patients with no medical training could later describe in exact detail the procedures used in resuscitation attempts while that patient appeared to the physician to be dead or in a coma.[24]

In *Reflections on Life after Life,* Moody describes four additional elements which a few subjects have mentioned but which he feels are common enough to merit attention. Some have told him that during their encounter with near death, they "got brief glimpses of an entire separate realm of existence in which all knowledge—whether of past, present, or future—seemed to co-exist in a sort of timeless state. Alternatively, this has been described as a moment of enlightenment in which the subject seemed to have complete knowledge."[25] However, these subjects commonly reported that a definite kind of special "forgetting" of this knowledge had to take place prior to their return to a normal, conscious existence.

Second, a number of individuals described finding themselves in a heavenly place or in the "cities of light" described previously on page 19.

A third new element involved the discovery by some of a realm of "bewildered spirits." These seemed to be deceased persons who were "unable to surrender their attachments to the physical world."[26] They are described as shuffling aimlessly about, having lost their identities. Some subjects thought that these "spirits" kept trying unsuccessfully to contact persons still physically alive.

The final new element concerns supernatural rescues. Some of Moody's subjects reported that they were saved from death by the intervention of a spiritual being. Many of these individuals attributed this intervention directly to God.

These four elements recently introduced by Moody appear to be, to some degree, extensions or elaborations of the first fifteen. None of them poses any apparent contradiction to Moody's previous writings.

**Moody's Conclusions**   After giving a number of illustrations and explanations of each of the various characteristics of near-death experiences, Moody makes a brief attempt to find parallels in earlier literature on death. He examines, for example, a few "parallel passages" in the Bible, the Dialogues of Plato, the Tibetan Book of the Dead and the writings of Emanuel Swedenborg, suggesting that there are many similarities between these writings and the descriptions of his patients.

A careful examination of these supposed parallels, however, quickly reveals that there are also many differences, not only differences in details but differences in world view and perspective. Moody, for example, makes no attempt to reconcile the discrep-

ancy between the apostle Paul's account of the resurrection body in 1 Corinthians 15 and the afterlife
visions of Plato in the myth of Ur in the *Republic*. In
the Bible there is a great respect for the continuity of
the resurrected body with the earthly body; in Plato
and also in Swedenborg there is a decided denegration of the body, a treatment of it as if it were the prison house of the soul rather than something so important that it is transformed and thus forever belongs to
a person.

Moody, however, seems not to recognize such differences but is content simply to draw the parallels
and make the general statement that all of these accounts "agree so well, both among themselves and
with the narratives of contemporary individuals who
have come as close as anyone alive to the state of
death."[27]

In both *Life after Life* and *Reflections on Life after
Life,* Moody is careful not to claim scientific objectiv-
ity: "What I have done here does not constitute a
scientific study. And to my fellow philosophers I
would insist that I am not under the delusion that I
have 'proven' there is life after death. . . . I refuse to
draw any 'conclusions' from my study and . . . I am
not trying to construct a proof of the ancient doctrine
of the survival of bodily death."[28] He leaves the reader, nonetheless, with the distinct impression that
there exists a large body of evidence which certainly
must be accounted for, and this might well lead to the
conclusion that there is life after life.

Dr. Elisabeth Kübler-Ross, who has contributed a
foreword to *Life after Life*, seems more convinced that
Moody has made a case. She writes, "It is research
such as Dr. Moody presents in his book that will en-

lighten many and will *confirm* what we have been taught for two thousand years—that there is life after death" (emphasis mine).[29] It is to her own contributions to this field of thanatology that we now turn.

# Beyond Death and Dying: Elisabeth Kübler-Ross

*3*

Undoubtedly the best-known thanatologist is physician and psychiatrist Dr. Elisabeth Kübler-Ross. Dr. Kübler-Ross has written a number of books based on her experience with terminally ill patients, the most respected being *On Death and Dying*.[1] Her work has proven extremely helpful in understanding the process which most people go through in their final stages of life.

She has not yet published any research concerned with experiences of people who have been clinically dead but subsequently revived. In a number of interviews and lectures, however, Dr. Kübler-Ross has indicated something of her views and current beliefs regarding life after death. In the last few years she has spoken widely throughout the world to many different groups of people who deal daily with death. In a recent interview with Ann Nietzke published in *Human Behavior* (September 1977) Dr. Kübler-Ross talked intimately and at length about her current work and relatively recent experience with dying patients and with the whole life-after-life phenomenon.[2] At the time of the interview, she was engaged in lecturing at the Toletine Ecumenical Center in Olympia Fields, Illinois.

**Beyond a Shadow of a Doubt**  Perhaps the most striking difference between the tone of Dr. Moody's work and the tone of Dr. Kübler-Ross's work is the certainty with which she speaks. "Undeniably," writes Nietzke, Dr. Kübler-Ross "speaks on the subject with the fervent conviction of one who knows without question that she is right."[3] Another interviewer likewise quotes Dr. Kübler-Ross, "I know beyond a shadow of a doubt that there is life after death. . . . For two thousand years, people have been told to believe in life after death. Now I say that we have evidence that this is true."[4] Dr. Kübler-Ross speaks of at least three kinds of evidence.

The *first* kind of evidence which Kübler-Ross gives parallels the work of Raymond Moody. Lennie Kronisch, the director of the Wholistic Health Institute in San Francisco, reports on one of Dr. Kübler-Ross's lectures:

We heard accounts [from Kübler-Ross] of patients who had been pronounced dead who inexplicbly [sic] returned to life minutes to hours later to describe what they had experienced. In hundreds of cases the description was the same: the sensation of floating up and out of the body like a butterfly shedding its cocoon; the witnessing of the death-bed scene, often involving the heroic efforts of doctors and nurses. Patients were able to describe minute details of events that took place—who was there, in what order they came into the room, what was said. Each reported that a life review took place, the proverbial "my life flashed before my eyes in an instant." Dr. Ross explained that in this dimension there is no element of time as we know it and indeed, one's life and all one's experiences as well as feelings and thoughts are literally re-run at once in a total cleansing purge. A profound sense of peace is felt, of light and beauty, of un-imagineable [sic] love. . . . All experienced themselves as whole and perfect and many expressed resentment at being "brought back" to their pained and diseased bodies. In each and every case the patient no longer felt any fear of death.[5]

In describing the reports of those who have been clin-ically dead and yet revived, Kübler-Ross mentions many of the components of this experience outlined by Moody. She becomes more explicit at times, in-dicating that "whomever you loved most in life and who has preceded you in death is there to help you make the transition."[6] When asked about hell, she explains, "The real hell comes after the initial transi-tion, when you are given a review of your own life—very much like watching it on television. You will then see all the times that you should have acted one way and you acted another; all the times you brought pain to others you will regret. It is not God who will convince you of your wrongs, but yourself. And it is hell."[7]

Concerning the connection between the body and

the soul (that is, the physical body and the "second body"), Elisabeth Kübler-Ross writes: "We have an umbilical cord, very like the one by which we are attached to our mothers. It connects us to our second body—the image that the consciousness carries of the physical self—and when we die, it is severed. People who drift in and out of comas are still attached by it to their bodies. Some persons . . . can actually see it—I cannot. . . . The Russians and those working with Krilian photography [a kind of photographic technique claiming to record the 'image' of the aura, or energy field, surrounding living beings] are trying to photograph this cord. When we can definitely say it exists, we will have a new definition of death."[8]

**Trips beyond Space and Time**  Dr. Kübler-Ross does not base her entire case for life after death on the reports of her patients' near-death experiences. There is a second kind of evidence. With Ann Nietzke she shared some of her own experiences which, while not near-death experiences, parallel them to a considerable degree. Her first out-of-the-body experience (OOBE) came "about three years ago" (1974?) when she was exhausted. During this experience she "suddenly felt herself separate from her body as 'a whole bunch of beings' began to work on it."[9] She awakened after a "beautiful two-hour sleep" and felt very refreshed and much younger. A woman who was with her at the time "told her that she had appeared dead— without pulse or respiration."[10]

After this experience, she got in touch with Robert A. Monroe whose investigation and experience with OOBEs I will examine in the next chapter. From him she learned how to have out-of-the-body experiences at will. In these experiences, she claims to have reached a place beyond space and time. During her first time in this realm all she could remember was the phrase Shanti Nilaya. Later she learned that this word means " 'ultimate home of peace,' which is where we all end up one day when we have gone through all the hell and all the agonies that life brings and have been able to accept it."[11]

In one of her most memorable journeys, she says that she experienced "every single death of every single one of my thousand patients. And I mean the physical pain, dyspnea, the agony, the screaming for help."[12] When she finally accepted the pain and agony as her own, she experienced "the most incredible rebirth experience."[13] This she describes in some detail concluding that the whole experience "was so incredibly beautiful that if I would describe it as 1,000 orgasms at one time it would be a very shabby comparison."[14] The next morning she says she walked outside and found herself "in love with every leaf, every tree, every bird—even the pebbles. I know I didn't walk on the pebbles but a little above them. I kept saying to the pebbles, 'I can't step on you because I can't hurt you.' They were alive as I was, and I was part of this whole alive universe."[15] Dr. Kübler-Ross has subsequently learned that she had experienced cosmic consciousness.

Her own OOBEs, then, constitute the second type of evidence explaining Kübler-Ross's certainty that there is life after death. Nietzke comments, "Although a mystical rebirth or 'cosmic consciousness' experience such as Elisabeth's certainly does not accompany or follow as a standard part of the typical OOBE, it has been found that people who have experienced themselves in the 'second' or 'spiritual' body no longer question the existence of an afterlife—they have experienced being alive and conscious outside the physical body and thus *know* they have some kind of soul that will transcend bodily death."[16]

**Visitations from the Other Side**     A *third* reason why Dr. Kübler-Ross is certain that there is an afterlife involves the materialization of a former patient of hers who had died and was buried. A Mrs. Schwartz appeared in Kübler-Ross's office as "her fully human self to thank Elisabeth for having taken care of her and to encourage her to continue her work with dying patients."[17] In order to test the reality of this apparition, Dr. Kübler-Ross "insisted that she write a note and sign it, a note that she says is now in the possession of a priest who had also worked with Mrs. Schwartz and who verified the handwriting."[18] That particular event occurred in 1969, just prior to the publication of *On Death and Dying*.

Finally, it is worth mentioning that in September 1976 Dr. Kübler-Ross came in contact with "spiritual guides" who "now appear to her often and serve her as her personal guides."[19] Lennie Kronisch says that in the Kübler-Ross lecture which she attended Dr. Ross said, "Last night I was visited by Salem, my spirit guide, and two of his companions, Anka and Willie. They were with us until three o'clock in the morning. We talked, laughed and sang together. They spoke and touched me with the most incredible love and tenderness imaginable. This was the highlight of my life."[20]

In summary, Kübler-Ross feels that her research with terminally ill patients indicates (1) that there is life after death, (2) that those who are clinically dead or in comas often have similar experiences to those described by Dr. Moody, (3) that we are attached to our physical bodies by a kind of spiritual umbilical cord even during OOBEs and that terminal death occurs when this cord is severed. Apparently she does not believe in a traditional heaven or a hell but rather that everyone after death enters into a very peaceful experience in the company of loved ones who have previously died and that people are "reborn," that is, reincarnated in another physical life at a later time.

It is obvious from the many lectures and interviews with Dr. Kübler-Ross that she has collected much material which she believes relates to life after death.[21] Until this is published (and there is an indication that she is working on such a publication) we must be content with relatively sketchy indications of her views. We know those of her recently acquired friend, Robert Monroe, much better.

# Journeys Out of the Body: Robert A. Monroe

# 4

Robert A. Monroe's book, *Journeys Out of the Body*, was published in 1971, and he appears to have been and to remain a significant influence on the thinking of both Moody and Kübler-Ross. Monroe does not deal directly with death and dying but rather with a series of fantastic personal out-of-the-body experiences.

**Up, Up and Away**   When his interest in OOBEs began, Monroe was a naturalist. "Religion," he states, "had not greatly influenced my thinking. . . . Beyond childhood churchgoing and rare attendance with a friend, God and church and religion had meant little to me. . . . It simply didn't evoke my interest."[1]

In 1958 this Virginia businessman who was "living a reasonably normal life with a reasonably normal family,"[2] was experimenting with learning during sleep states. One Sunday while his family was at church, he was listening to a "relaxation" tape and, in the aftermath, experienced severe cramps. He suspected that this was somehow related to his efforts at concentration. Three weeks later on another Sunday afternoon he was taking a nap. Suddenly he seemed to be struck by a beam of warm light which caused his entire body to vibrate or shake violently.

These episodes began to happen frequently until one evening during such an experience it seemed to him that without conscious effort his fingers and hand were slipping through the rug and then the floor beneath as though no physical impediment existed. Puzzled and believing that he had had a hallucination, Monroe cautiously pursued more experimentation with this strange phenomenon.

One night he found himself "floating against the ceiling, bouncing gently with any movement I made. I rolled in the air, startled, and looked down. There, in the dim light below me, was the bed. There were two figures lying in the bed. To the right was my wife. Beside her was someone else. Both seemed asleep. . . . I looked more closely, and the shock was intense. I was the someone on the bed!"[3] Monroe thought that he was dying. "Desperately, like a diver, I swooped down to my body and dove in."[4]

As the weeks and months went by, Monroe gradually lost his fear of such OOBEs and began actively to seek them. He looked for ways in which to induce the "vibrations" associated with the exit from his physical body and sought to push beyond the limits of previous "journeys." His book describes many bizarre and curious OOBEs, all of which are incredible and some of which boggle the mind. He tells of encountering intelligent, nonhuman "things," of visiting a strange, otherworldly civilization and of nonphysical "sexual" charges exchanged with others in the "Second State" or nonphysical second body.

**The Search for an Explanation**   Monroe began to search for an intellectual framework by which he might understand what was happening to him. Biblical and Christian writings "did nothing but add to the conflict," but, he writes, "in the Eastern religions I found more acceptance of the idea."[5] Still, Monroe feels that the Bible makes reference to OOBEs if read from a point of view sympathetic to such experiences. He found that an "underground" existed in the United States whose members included psychics, astrologers and mediums, all of whom share an interest in the mysteries of the "Inner Self." Edgar Cayce, for example, Monroe dubs a "latter-day saint in the psychic world." "Most definitely," he writes, referring to Cayce's work, "here was truth unfolding."[6]

Monroe's curiosity about his new-found ability led him into varied experimentation. He once visited a medium. According to Monroe, spirit guides took over her body. Claiming to be her dead husband and an American Indian, they spoke through her. At first he discounted such guides simply as manifestations of a split personality in the medium. Shortly thereafter, however, he was visited by two ghostly figures and taken in the Second State to a séance. Later he checked the accuracy of his observations during this spirit trip by talking to several people whom he had seen participating in the séance. After that he resolved to keep a more open mind concerning spirit guides.

As his investigations continued, Monroe came into contact with others he had known who were now deceased. He tells of successfully attempting, while in the Second State, to meet his father, who had recently died. He found his father in a very small room in a place much like a hospital. His father was surprised to see him and they experienced a joyful reunion. However, for some unexplained reason, Monroe wondered if he should ever try to "see" his father again.

**Other Places, Other Spaces**  Monroe often wondered why in his journeys he found "no evidence to substantiate the biblical notions of God and afterlife in a place called heaven."[7] He did visit a place he terms "Locale II" and participated in some rather startling events:

In the midst of normal activity, whatever it may be, there is a distant Signal, almost like heraldic trumpets. Everyone takes the Signal calmly, and with it, everyone stops speaking or whatever he may be doing. It is the Signal that He (or They) is coming through His Kingdom. . . . At the Signal, each living thing lies down—my impression is on their backs, bodies arched to expose the abdomen . . . , with head turned to one side so that one does not see Him as He passes by. The purpose seems to be to form a living road over which He can travel. . . . In the several times that I have experienced this, I lay down with the others. At the time, the thought of doing otherwise was inconceivable. As He passes, there is a roaring musical sound and a feeling of radiant, irresistible living force of ultimate power that peaks overhead and fades in the distance. . . . Is this God? Or God's son? Or His representative?[8]

Monroe says that three times he want to a "place" which he equates with nirvana, the Samadhi and possibly the Christian heaven. "This is home," he felt. Each time he wanted to stay; each time he returned to this waking world he wanted to go back.[9]

Monroe also reports meeting someone who bears a resemblance to Moody's "being of light": "I immediately felt myself in the presence of someone standing there. I sensed his presence rather than saw him (impression, male). For some unaccountable reason that I do not yet understand, even recollected now in tranquility, I dropped thankfully in front of him and sobbed."[10]

**God: Revised Version**   Eventually, based upon further OOBEs, Monroe revised his view of God. He describes being visited by an intelligent force who seemed to be examining his mind in order to understand how humans existed in earth's atmosphere. He tells us, "I mentally (orally also?) asked who they were, and received an answer that I could not translate or understand. Then I felt them beginning to leave, and I asked for some actual indication that they had been there, but was rewarded only with paternal amusement." Their intelligence was far beyond human intelligence, he says, impersonal and cold, "with none of the emotions of love or compassion which we respect so much." Yet, Monroe conjectures, "This may be the omnipotence we call God. Visits such as these in mankind's past could well have been the basis for all of our religious beliefs, and our knowledge today could provide no better answers than we could a thousand years past."[11]

The effect on Monroe was profound: "I sat down and cried, great deep sobs as I have never cried before, because then I knew without any qualification or future hope of change that the God of my childhood, of the churches, of religion throughout the world was not as we worshiped him to be—that for the rest of my life, I would 'suffer' the loss of this illusion."[12]

**A New Humanity for a New Age**    After some attempts to describe how the reader can achieve OOBEs for himself, Monroe offers several premises. It is his belief that extensive research into the Second State could be the beginning of a new era in human history. He notes that an organized group of individuals who can operate in the Second State "could control the destiny of mankind."[13] To illustrate this he refers to an OOBE in which he pinched a lady and later verified with her that indeed she had suffered such a pinch during the time in question. Monroe then suggests that an individual during an OOBE could pinch a cerebral artery in the brain of a world leader causing him to suffer a stroke. Or he could save the life of another by pinching off a hemorrhaging brain artery. "All that is needed is the ability and the intent. If there are restraints or deterrents to such possible action, they are not apparent."[14] He also states that individuals operating in the Second State can affect humans mentally by, for example, causing them to experience "unaccounted-for compulsions, fears, neuroses, or irrational actions."[15]

If such research concerning OOBEs is undertaken

by "sophisticated man," man will be freed of all uncertainty of his relationship with God. His position relative to nature and the universe will be unequivocal knowledge. He will know, rather than believe, whether death is a passing or a finality. With such knowledge and expanded experience, religious conflict will be impossible. Quite probably, Catholics, Protestants, Jews, Hindus, Buddhists, et al. will still retain much of their individuality, knowing that each has its place in Locale II. ... Man would then proceed systematically with his preparation for life in Locale II on a sound basis, liberated from the misinterpretation of distorted visions subjectively experienced and/or observed by uninformed and relatively uneducated fanatics many centuries ago. In so doing, he may have to face facts both unpalatable and uncomfortable. Traditional concepts of good and bad, right and wrong will undoubtedly be subject to radical redefinition. The truth may indeed hurt for a generation or so.[16]

Robert Monroe has since begun to initiate just such research at his headquarters near Charlottesville, Virginia, which is known as "M-5000." The function of this organization is to teach clients how to achieve OOBEs using a series of tape recordings which utilize delta-theta pulsing, plus a binaural beat, in combination with voice-over relaxation instructions. Tal Brooke, who participated in Monroe's investigations in the 1960s, reports in an interview that Monroe evolved a tape technique by receiving instructions from various spirit guides.[17]

## The Moody, Kübler-Ross, Monroe Connection  A

direct connection has been reported between Monroe and Kübler-Ross. "Kübler-Ross serves on the board of advisors for M-5000 and occasionally (if not regularly) refers clients to Monroe."[18] "She has herself undergone the OBE training twice, reportedly getting out of her body on both occasions."[19]

It is also of interest to note that in addition to his work with Monroe, Tal Brooke was also "a friend and fellow student of Moody at the University of Virginia. At the time Brooke was an avid and omnivorous student of esoteric philosophies, whether Eastern-religious, occult or psychic. This was a fascination which Moody shared, and this common interest was, in fact, the major basis for their companionship. Brooke (who later became a Christian in India in 1971) relates that Moody claimed that he regularly conversed with a spirit being (which he identified as 'God') who manifested primarily as a voice in his head."[20]

Thus we see the influence of Monroe on Kübler-Ross and Moody. Moody and Kübler-Ross work closely with one another and, according to Albrecht and Alexander, both work closely with Monroe and his investigations.[21] We must now examine the findings of these three investigators in the light of the biblical view of death.

# Testing
# the Spirits:
# An Evaluation

**5**

What are we to make of all these near-death experiences and their apparent near relatives, the OOBEs, occurring without the proximity of death? Were the patients near death ever really dead? If so, when did their "experience" come? Before death as perhaps the mind made a last-ditch stand against threatened annihilation or threatened punishment? Or after revival as the mind-brain attempted to supply an explanation for its resuscitation?

Are we to accept them as veridical accounts of journeys to other actual places or spaces in God's universe, his heaven or his hell? Or are they hallucinations brought about by a malfunctioning brain—dreams that somehow take on the appearance of reality? If they are hallucinations, how are they triggered? By physical causes (exhaustion, chemical imbalance in the brain, injury to the brain tissue)? Or by demonic spiritual forces wishing to delude us? Is it possible that some are veridical and some deceptions? If so, how are we, viewing them from the outside, able to tell?

What if you or I were to experience an OOBE? How could we tell the difference between a journey to heaven and a journey to a place that looks like we think heaven might be (whatever we think about that subject)?

These are only some of the rabbits we have flushed from the field. They are all very vexing questions, and our answers to many of them must be tentative. To the most important of these questions, however, I believe there are some clear answers. Let us take up first the question of death itself.

**What Is Death?**    The first question that we are likely to ask regarding near-death experiences is whether any of the patients who reported journeying to the other side were actually dead. The reason for this is that, as Moody points out, "as long as it remains a possibility that there was some residual biological activity in the body, then that activity might have caused, and thus account for, the experience."[1] In other words, these visions of the other side may be mere hallucinations of a mind struggling to bring order out of a malfunctioning brain. The question is, then, what is death?

Moody gives three possible definitions of death. First, death has traditionally been conceived of as the absence of clinically detectable vital signs. When there are no such vital signs, the patient is said to be "clinically dead." Evidence of clinical death includes lack of heartbeat and breathing for an extended period of time, blood pressure dropping so low as to be unreadable, dilated pupils and falling body temperature. On this basis, Moody says that many of the patients to whom he spoke were certainly dead: "Both the testimony of physicians and the evidence of medical records adequately support the contention that 'death' in this sense did take place."[2]

A second definition of death is the absence of any brain wave activity. If the electroencephalograph (EEG) gives a "flat" reading, it is assumed that there is no activity in the brain. But, Moody comments, the EEG is hard to use accurately, and even if these patients had been properly prepared with the machine in operation, there could be doubt as to the accuracy of the readings. In any case, John Weldon and Zola Levitt report that "flat EEG readings . . . have gone on for 24 hours in patients who then completely recovered."[3] Moreover, as pointed out above, so long as the person actually did revive, there would always be a question as to whether the experience of death took place on either edge and not during the time of the "flat" EEG.

The third definition of death is that it is "an irreversible loss of vital functions" (Moody's language) or "that state in which physical resuscitation is impossible" (Weldon and Levitt's language).[4] According to this definition, regardless of clinical death or a flat EEG, a person is not dead unless he does not revive. In this sense none of Moody's patients was actually dead.

As Christians, we might find it useful to adopt this definition of death. John Weldon and Zola Levitt in

fact do so. This would allow us to discount any of
the stories as being veridical concerning death. We
would still be challenged to explain them, but we
would not have to bother with the possible conflict
between the supposed experiences of death and the
testimony of Scripture. We would know already that
what was reported as happening after death did not
happen after death at all.

There is, however, a serious problem in adopting
this definition of death: the scriptural accounts of
death and resuscitation would need to be reinter-
preted, perhaps even demythologized. For example,
in 1 Kings 17:17-24, Elijah revived a boy whose
"sickness was so severe, that there was no breath left
in him" (v. 17). Elijah carried the boy into his own
room, stretched himself out upon him three times
and called to the Lord, "O LORD my God, I pray Thee,
let this child's life return to him" (v. 21). And the
writer comments, "And the life of the child returned
to him and he revived" (v.22).

Likewise 2 Kings 4:18-37 recounts a resuscitation
of a young boy by Elisha. The boy had become ill in
the fields during harvest and was taken to his mother:
"He sat on her lap until noon, and then died" (v. 20).
Elisha had to be summoned from quite a distance, and
so the boy must have lain for hours in this condition.
Moreover, it took some time for the resuscitation to
take place. Finally, Elisha "put his mouth on his
mouth and his eyes on his eyes and his hands on his
hands, and he stretched himself on him; and the flesh
of the child became warm. Then he returned and
walked in the house once back and forth, and went up
and stretched himself on him; and the lad sneezed
seven times and the lad opened his eyes" (vv. 34-35).

The New Testament also contains such accounts. As Jesus was approaching the city of Nain, "a dead man was being carried out" (Lk. 7:12). Jesus commanded him, "Young man, I say to you, arise!" and then "the dead man sat up, and began to speak" (Lk. 7:14-15). Then, of course, there was Lazarus (Jn. 11: 1-45). Jesus plainly declared, "Lazarus is dead" (v. 14). And of course Martha insisted that he couldn't be alive, saying, "Lord, by this time there will be a stench; for he *has been dead* four days" (v. 39). Nonetheless, Jesus raised Lazarus from the dead.

Later Jesus' disciples were to raise at least two people from the dead. First there was Dorcas (Acts 9:36-43) who "fell sick and died" (v. 37) but was raised by the apostle Peter. And there was also Eutychus (Acts 20:7-12) who fell asleep on a windowsill on the third floor and tumbled out. He was "picked up dead" (v. 9), but Paul embraced him and revived him, saying, "Do not be troubled, for his life is in him" (v. 10). Indeed, the boy lived.[5]

From a biblical standpoint, then, it appears inappropriate to define death as a state in which resuscitation is impossible. However convenient it might be to us (allowing us, for example, to discount any near-death experience as totally void of any epistemological value), as Christians we must stick with our best understanding of Scripture.

Finally, Moody suggests a fourth definition of death: "Let us . . . hypothesize that death is a separation of the mind from the body, and that the mind does pass into other realms of existence at this point."[6] This definition squares well with the notion of the "silver cord" mentioned by Kübler-Ross and Monroe. When that cord is shattered, then re-entry into the body is not possible and the soul (or second body) takes on a separate existence. This definition is a speculative conclusion more than an observation. As such it is of a different order from the first three definitions and does not conflict with any of them. Nonetheless, while this definition might be true, it is difficult to see how it could help determine the death of a patient. How are we to know whether the spirit has indeed left the body for good?

So where does this leave us? What after all is death? Oddly enough, despite the long analysis, I am going to argue that the definition of death is not really vital to our discussion. The reason is this. Even if those patients whom Moody has interviewed did die, and even if their experience occurred during the time of their death and was remembered after they were revived, the stories which they bring back are not necessarily veridical. There is no reason why what they experienced could not be as illusory or deceitful as a hallucination produced by a malfunctioning brain. We are a gullible people. We tend to believe that anything visionary and mystical which happens outside of the body is necessarily true. We are more prone to mistrust our five senses than we are the mind's interpretations. But this lack of skepticism with regard to mystical experience (that is, experience out of the body or purely mental experience) is not necessarily justified. If, apart from the experience itself, there are good reasons why we should be skeptical of the experience, then we should at least suspend judgment until we evaluate those reasons.

**The Truth about Reality**   Whether the near-death

experiences took place prior to death, during death or after resuscitation, we still need to ask whether those experiences tell us anything true about reality. In other words, even if we could demonstrate that the near-death experiences occurred during death, we would have to evaluate the character of those experiences and determine whether they provide insight into the way things really are.

In order to clarify the issues, it is necessary to differentiate between (1) observations or data simply described by those who experienced them, (2) interpretations applied to these observations and experienced by those subjects or patients providing the data, (3) conclusions drawn from either observations or interpreted experiences by either the patients or the investigators and (4) the values, beliefs, biases and assumptions of the investigators which either predated their research or were developed as a result of their work. Such assumptions certainly would be expected to color their ultimate published conclusions and the direction of their future research.

Much of the observational data is interesting and could provide some clues concerning life hereafter. Nonetheless, it is obvious from even a cursory survey of the whole body of material that some of it conflicts with biblical teaching. So, for us as Christians the question is this: Are the reported descriptive observations (the basic data provided by the subjects of the research) in conflict with biblical truth? Or are *only* the interpretations of the data, the conclusions and biases of the patients and/or investigators inconsistent with scriptural teaching while the basic data in and of itself is not?

Ineffability, the first characteristic of near-death

experiences, is found in the writings of the apostle Paul. Probably speaking of himself, Paul said: "I know a man in Christ who fourteen years ago— whether in the body I do not know, or out of the body I do not know, God knows—such a man was caught up to the third heaven. And I know how such a man—whether in the body or apart from the body I do not know, God knows—was caught up into Paradise, and heard inexpressible words, which a man is not permitted to speak" (2 Cor. 12:2-4). Paul feels no compulsion to explain what he finds inexplicable. The ineffability of the near-death experience may frustrate our curiosity, but it is not in conflict with biblical revelation.

Likewise, various other experiences (hearing oneself pronounced dead, entering a dark void or tunnel and being rapidly transported into an environment of peace and tranquility) do not appear to contradict any biblical teachings. Paul, or the man to whom he was referring in the Corinthian passage, certainly experienced some sense of being transported out of his physical body into another realm, and this was not in any way considered wrong or prohibited.

The Kübler-Ross theory positing a spiritual umbilical cord connecting the soul or spiritual being with the physical being during such an OOBE does not appear to be in conflict with the Bible.[7] In fact it may have some scriptural support. Ecclesiastes 12:6-7 may be applicable: "Remember Him before *the silver cord is broken* and the golden bowl is crushed, the pitcher by the well is shattered and the wheel at the cistern is crushed; then the dust will return to the earth as it was, and the spirit will return to God who gave it" (emphasis mine). Of course, if such literalism is followed consistently, we would need to find correlates for the golden bowl, the pitcher, the wheel and the well. Still, there is a striking, even if accidental, parallel to the testimony of those who have had OOBEs.[8]

Although it may be possible to reconcile the idea of a spiritual umbilical cord with the Bible, it is not possible to go the next further step with Kübler-Ross and thus to share her de-emphasis on the physical body. She, along with Monroe and Moody, seems to promote the notion that the body is only the prison of the soul and, therefore, that it is good to escape it forever. This is actually a Platonic concept, also found widely in occult philosophy, apparently being revived by these investigators. The idea is alien to the Bible in that the Scriptures teach that the separation of the body from the spirit and soul is an unnatural condition and will be rectified with the eventual resurrection of the body. This resurrection body will be in many ways different from our present physical body, but a body it will be nonetheless. Jesus' resurrected body serves as an indication of what our resurrected bodies will be like. Kübler-Ross is, however, consistent in that such a de-emphasis on the body is necessary for one who believes in reincarnation, that is, that we all will have had and will have discarded several physical bodies.[9]

**Other People, Other Spirits**    It is at the point where people having OOBEs report meeting other people and other spirits that we begin to encounter puzzles in relation to the teachings of the Bible. Moody's patients and Monroe and Kübler-Ross themselves report seeing or sensing others in spiritual form who have come to help them or to reassure them. Who are these beings?

It is no mere coincidence that this is the first juncture at which interpretation begins to be applied to observation in more than a simple, descriptive manner. If we identify these beings as deceased relatives or past acquaintances, we move from the realm of simple description and enter the realm of interpretation. What are the possibilities? Who might these beings be?

Leaving aside, for the moment, the question of the identity of the being of light and concentrating only on the other spiritual beings, we have several possibilities. First, they could be the departed spirits of those who have died before. This is the usual interpretation of those who have had OOBEs. Is there any biblical warrant for this possibility?

The answer is yes, but with an important proviso. Contact or communication between those who are alive and those who are dead is strictly forbidden. The law as expressed in Deuteronomy 18:10-12 is as follows: "There shall not be found among you anyone who makes his son or his daughter pass through the fire, one who uses divination, one who practices witchcraft, or one who interprets omens, or a sorcerer, or one who casts a spell, or a medium, or a spiritist, or one who calls up the dead. For whoever does these things is detestable to the LORD; and because of these detestable things the LORD your God will drive them out before you."

Nonetheless, the Bible records an instance of an individual speaking with the spirit of a deceased human being. King Saul of Israel consulted a medium in order to call up the dead Samuel. Samuel did appear—a great surprise to the medium who perhaps was expecting a familiar spirit disguised as Samuel. But Saul was severely punished for putting his hope in a medium: "So Saul died for his trespass which he committed against the LORD, because of the word of the LORD which he did not keep; and also because he asked counsel of a medium, making inquiry *of it*, and did not inquire of the LORD. Therefore He killed him, and turned the kingdom to David the son of Jesse" (1 Chron. 10:13-14).

It would seem to be easy to generalize from these passages that the Bible forbids all contact with the dead, but before we do we must consider the transfiguration. Jesus took Peter, James and John up on a high mountain and was transfigured so that "His face shone like the sun, and His garments became as white as light. And behold, Moses and Elijah appeared to them, talking with Him" (Mt. 17:2-3). On the way down the mountain, Jesus specifically commanded his companions not to tell anyone about the vision until after his resurrection. It is obvious that this is a special occasion involving a special person, God incarnate, and that it is not to be taken as normative for human experience.

The conclusion, therefore, from a biblical standpoint is that contact with the dead may under rare  circumstances occur, but under no circumstances is it to be sought. Perhaps one reason for this is that human beings can easily be persuaded that they are having contact with the dead—their friends and relatives who have preceded them—when in fact they are having contact with spiritual beings who are impersonating them. But this is to jump ahead in the argument. We must first consider another possibility.

A second possibility is that these reported experiences have a neurological basis and are hallucinations or images produced by tapping into the memory banks of the brain. Albrecht and Alexander say, "If studies which estimate that we use only 10% of our mental capacity are correct, the other 90% must be capable of incredible things if the right 'buttons' are pushed, including the virtual re-experiencing of authentic life-memories. All of this is to suggest that while these experiences are real enough, they may display the potential of the human nervous system rather than the nature of the 'other side.' "[10]

Another similar explanation which has received a great deal of attention in the past few years is related to the use of hallucinogenic drugs. It is commonly reported that even in the pre-Columbian era, the Aztec Indians were chewing the buds of the peyote plant in order to induce religious visions. A revival of sorts has taken place in the use of peyote by some Indian groups. "After eating the sacred peyote, the Indians see visions similar to those seen by the clinically dead, those experiencing near-death, and those traveling out-of-body," writes Wheeler.[11] Wheeler comments, "A separation of body and soul similar to that felt by those who have touched death for a moment is clearly part of the Indian religious experience."[12] And he concludes, "Indian mythology and legends may be as close to the truth about the hereafter as reports of the Other Side learned from the out-of-body travelers."[13] Perhaps, then, all near-death experiences are most parsimoniously explained as the result of brain chemistry associated with the use of mind-bending drugs, or as another investigator has suggested, the "effects of psychochemicals such as $CO_2$ on still-living brain cells during the dying process."[14]

Those familiar with hypnosis are aware that subjects in a trance state can be directed to imagine in visual and verbal imagery the most fantastic scenes and that those subjects are often quite capable of creating such a scene and expanding creatively upon it. While so doing, the environment their brain has created or caused them to "see" is very real to them; it is as though they were actually there, though they have never left the room. When, as one example, such a subject is asked to imagine that he has suddenly been transformed into a tiny blood cell traveling along his own vascular system and then is asked to describe the journey as it progresses, very interesting descriptions may be obtained. Such brain imagery might account for some of the reported observations by the three major investigators. Of course, it does not fully explain some of Monroe's contacts with other humans also living at the time who he feels later validated his observations during a journey in the Second State. It also does not fully account for some of the experiences of Kübler-Ross's and Moody's patients, especially those associated with details of the events taking place in the operating room while the patient was unconscious, if not clinically dead.

To me, a more persuasive alternative is to accept these reported experiences as real encounters, not however as encounters with loved ones or former patients in spirit form, but rather as encounters with beings who counterfeited those loved ones, that is, who looked and sounded familiar. This would sound wildly fantastic except for the biblical warnings which indicate that this is well within the limits of the power of Satan and the spirits under his command. Even Monroe seems to recognize that such deception as this is possible although he fails to carry this insight to its logical conclusion and thus to question many, if not all, of his observations, conclusions and interpretations.

Monroe reports one rather frightening "trip" which clearly illustrates the possibilities for this type of satanic illusion. As he began one of his OOBEs, he felt something—which he describes as "humanoid"—climb on his back. As he tried to pull it off, if felt "rubbery." The "little fellow" stretched as he pulled. Finally he succeeded in removing it, but it seemed determined to climb back on top of him.

I tried to stay calm, but it wasn't easy. I crossed myself several times, with no effect. I repeated the Lord's Prayer fervently, but that didn't hold him at bay; then I screamed for help.

Then, as I was trying to hold off the first, a second climbed on my back! . . . I got a good look at each, and as I looked, each turned into a good facsimile of one of my two daughters (the psychiatrists will have a good time with this one)! I seemed to know immediately that *this was a deliberate camouflage on their parts* to create emotional confusion in me and call upon my love for my daughters to prevent my doing anything more to them.

The moment I realized the trick, the two *no longer appeared to be my daughters.*[15] (Emphasis mine.)

It would be consistent with the Bible to accept as valid the reported experiences of those clinically dead who later claimed to have encountered other spirit beings. I would understand from the Scriptures that these beings are angels and may either be servants of God or demons. It is not necessary to accept the interpretation that these are disembodied spirits of deceased relatives in order to believe that those individuals did, indeed, sense or see spirits who appeared to be people known to them. I believe that these particular beings who appeared as loved ones were really demons masquerading as loved ones in order to deceive the person into believing false doctrines and discarding biblical authority. This will be noted as a pattern or consistent result which emerges from accepting at face value the interpretations placed on observations on which the life-after-life research is based.

I do not wish to imply that after we die we do not join loved ones and friends, assuming all are Christians. Then, too, there may be some who would suggest that God may occasionally give one of his children a very special gift, perhaps when that person is dying—a gift of "seeing" a loved one who has gone on before. It might be suggested that since that person did not seek such an experience and did not receive a message contrary to the Scripture, that it is not in violation of the clear and strong biblical prohibition against mediumistic activities. Indeed, Ralph Wilkerson, chancellor of Melodyland School of Theology and a well-known evangelist with a healing ministry, reports a number of near-death experiences of born-again Christians. Marvin Ford, for example, entered a splendid city, "saw its gates of pearl, its streets of gold . . . [and] viewed its walls of jasper." Then he saw a "resplendent light" he identified as Jesus.[16]

However, in view of the scriptural warnings, such

experiences must be interpreted very cautiously. If such "visions" do occur within God's will, then it is clear that they will in no way lead the visionary to accept new ideas in violation of scriptural teachings or to discard biblical doctrines. Such a "vision" could only be seen in the context of a hypothesis—such as Dr. Vernon Grounds has mentioned—that dying is a process, much as is birth.[17] One assumption that might follow from such a hypothesis would be that God may help individuals through that process in special and unique ways. Again, it would also follow, that whatever methods he might use during such a process would in no way violate his own Word, the Bible.

As C. Stephen Board says, "If the message about death [given us in the Bible] is true, the contradictory message of some of Moody's patients cannot be true. Their experiences may be authentic, and they may be honest reporters of those experiences, but the intellectual cargo, the 'teaching' about God and an afterlife without judgment, must be either a mistake or a deception."[18]

**The Being of Light**   By far the most crucial element in Moody's research is his patients' encounters with what he terms the "being of light." It is crucial because, based upon this particular portion of their experience and the information given to them by this mysterious and attractive personality, they later draw conclusions which directly contradict basic biblical doctrines and teachings.

The observation datum is that of meeting a light which has a definite personality almost overwhelmingly warm and accepting. The interpretation usually placed upon this observation is that this person or being is someone good or positive, someone *who can be totally trusted.* The conclusion drawn from this interpretation or identification by both patients and research investigators is that the information imparted to them from this being, either overtly or by implication, is completely reliable and true and can, therefore, be used to form the basis of a life philosophy and the setting of goals when one returns to the physical body. In fact, this being is assumed to be so beyond question that other sources of authority, such as the Bible, can be safely discarded.

The Bible certainly would not lead us to question or reject the report that these individuals have, in fact, encountered a very special, very attractive presence or personality to whom they felt immediately drawn in a very positive way. However, we can and should be skeptical as to the identification of that personality and the conclusions which logically follow. The Scriptures describe a number of spiritual personalities who we assume would be awesomely attractive if we were to encounter them.

First, the Bible describes moments of encounter between humans and angels sent as messengers from God during which people were overwhelmed and experienced a very bright light. According to Luke an "angel of the Lord" came to the shepherds at Jesus' birth, and "the glory of the Lord shone around them; and they were terribly frightened" (Lk. 2:9). The Gospel of Matthew recounts that at the resurrection, an "angel of the Lord descended from heaven. . . . His appearance was like lightning, and his garment white as snow; and the guards shook for fear of him" (Mt. 28:2-4).

Second, we note, as did Moody, that when Paul was confronted by Jesus on the road to Damascus, "a very bright light suddenly flashed from heaven all around" Paul (Acts 22:6). Jesus' appearance in the book of Revelation is also startling: "His eyes were like a flame of fire; . . . and his face was like the sun shining in its strength" (Rev. 1:14, 16).

Third, one other important being is also described in terms that might surprise us, for we have often been taught to think of him quite differently—usually in terms of a pitchfork and a pointed tail. In the Old Testament book of Isaiah, Satan is described as an extremely beautiful creature:

How you are fallen from heaven,
O star of the morning, son of the dawn!
You have been cut down to the earth,
You who have weakened the nations!
But you said in your heart,
"I will ascend to heaven;
I will raise my throne above the stars of God,
And I will sit on the mount of assembly
In the recesses of the north.
I will ascend above the heights of the clouds;
I will make myself like the Most High."
(Is. 14:12-14)

The Bible teaches that the devil, also referred to as Satan or Lucifer, was a very beautiful angel, so intelligent, powerful and attractive that he presumed to rebel against his Creator and attempted to become like God or to become his own god. Satan's principal agenda in his relationship with the human race since Eve and Adam has been to seduce us into the same rebellion for the same end—to be our own god, rejecting any need for a Savior or Messiah.

We note that Moody's patients were told by the being of light that their task in life was to love others and to gain knowledge. He did not mention that they should seek a relationship to God through Jesus, which the Bible states is the only way that we can really know how to love or even to truly know anything at all. It is interesting that when Satan tempted Eve in the garden of Eden, he offered her knowledge. He told her that if she would rebel against God and eat that which God had forbidden, her eyes would be opened and she would be like God (Gen. 3:5). Satan's basic plan of attack seems to be much the same whether described in Genesis, Isaiah or by our own temptations: rebel and seek knowledge above all else so that you too can be your own god.

Albrecht and Alexander sum up Satan's ploys this way:

> Biblically speaking, we know by revelation that the nature of our spiritual warfare as Christians is determined by a clash of *personal* wills—God's will vs. that of His adversary. The implications of this are that "evil" should be seen not as some impersonal negativity (like inertia or entropy) but as embodied in a corrupt personal entity possessing intelligence and will. This entity exists in dimensions beyond the space-time realm we live in, but is capable of interacting with it. Since it possesses *purposes,* this entity is quite capable of acting *strategically* in behalf of hidden objectives—i.e., deceitfully.[19]

Jesus spoke very forcefully about Satan's nature: "He was a murderer from the beginning, and does not stand in the truth, because there is no truth in him. Whenever he speaks a lie, he speaks from his own *nature; for he is a liar, and the father of lies"* (Jn. 8:44). Paul warned the early Christians repeatedly about the danger of deception by Satan. Speaking of those in opposition to true doctrine, he writes, "Perhaps God may grant them repentance leading to the knowledge of the truth, and they may come to their senses *and escape* from the snare of the devil, having been held captive by him to do his will" (2 Tim. 2:25-26).

Perhaps the most startling picture of Satan, relative to the life-after-life research, is found in Paul's second letter to the Corinthians. In discussing the lengths to which the devil can and will go to deceive both Christians and nonbelievers, Paul states that "Satan *disguises* himself as an *angel of light*" (2 Cor. 11:14, emphasis mine). The Authorized Version reads that Satan is "transformed" into an angel of light. So when people encounter a being of light whom they identify as Christ or an angel of God, it is quite possible that they, in fact, are encountering a very clever counterfeit—Satan or an angel of Satan in disguise. What appears to be light is not always light and what appears to be knowledge is not always knowledge.[20]

**A Contrary Gospel**   Since the Bible clearly warns us that this deception is possible, that we could mistake Satan for an angel of light, how can we distinguish between an encounter with Jesus or an angel of God on the one hand and encountering the devil or his angels disguised as beings of light on the other hand? Can we determine whether Moody's and Kübler-Ross's patients have talked with God or agents of God or have been seduced by the father of lies?

The Scriptures themselves give us guidance. We

know that "all Scripture is inspired by God and profitable for teaching for reproof, for correction, for training in righteousness" (2 Tim. 3:16). God cannot lie; he cannot contradict himself. Therefore, if we are to accept what a being of light speaks or otherwise communicates to us, whatever that being states or implies must be in perfect agreement with the Bible. If discord or contradiction exists between what such a being teaches and what the Scriptures teach, we are admonished to reject that being as false, as an agent of Satan—or perhaps even as Satan himself. We are told to choose the guidance of the Bible over and above *any* experiences we may have, even those experiences that are exceptional above and beyond our wildest imagination.

Paul, who himself apparently experienced an out-of-the-body trip, was quite prophetic in light of the Moody and Kübler-Ross writings and conclusions when he wrote to Christians almost two thousand years ago: "There are some who are disturbing you, and want to distort the gospel of Christ. But even though we, *or an angel from heaven,* should preach to you a gospel contrary to that which we have preached to you, let him be accursed" (Gal. 1:7-8, emphasis mine). He goes on to say that he was not taught the gospel by man but "*I received it* through a revelation of Jesus Christ" (Gal. 1:12). If the word "truth" is to have any meaning, Jesus could not have taught one truth to Paul and, as a being of light, teach a different truth to Moody's patients.

The being of light that many individuals in Moody's sample encountered either made direct propositions or left those individuals with definite assumptions that are in clear conflict with the Bible, not only with the teachings of Paul but with the Scriptures taken as a whole. The Bible, including the teachings of Jesus, indicates that those who have accepted Jesus as their Savior have no reason to fear death. They will not be condemned for their sins or rebellion against God because of Christ's substitutionary atonement for that sin. They will be judged as perfect, that is, as wrapped in Christ's perfection before God: "There is therefore now no condemnation for those who are in Christ Jesus" (Rom. 8:1). However, those who do not accept Jesus as Savior and Lord have every reason to be terrified of death, for they shall stand before God in judgment. Jesus said, speaking of himself: "He who believes in Him is not judged [or condemned]; he who does not believe has been judged already, because he has not believed in the name of the only begotten Son of God" (Jn. 3:18).

Moody indicates that almost every person he interviewed expressed to him that he or she was no longer afraid of death. Part of this change in attitude was due to the reassurance given by the being of light. Moody's interviewees also, for the most part, "abandoned and disavowed" the "reward-punishment model of the afterlife."[21] They found that the being of light responded only with "understanding and even with humor" when their "most apparently awful and sinful deeds were made manifest" before him.[22] Moody states, "In place of this old model, many seem to have returned with a new model and a new understanding of the world beyond—a vision which features not unilateral judgment, but rather cooperative development towards the ultimate end of self-realization."[23]

In sharp contrast, Jesus taught a "grace-punish-

ment model" involving heaven and hell. Speaking
again of himself, Jesus said in one prophetic statement, "Then He will also say to those on His left, 'De-
part from Me, accursed ones, into the eternal fire
which has been prepared for the devil and his angels.'
... These will go away into eternal punishment, but
the righteous into eternal life" (Mt. 25:41, 46). And
Paul writes, "The Lord Jesus shall be revealed from
heaven with His mighty angels in flaming fire, deal-
ing out retribution to those who do not know God and
to those who do not obey the gospel of our Lord Jesus.
And these will pay the penalty of eternal destruction,
away from the presence of the Lord and from the glory
of His power" (2 Thess. 1:7-9).

It becomes impossible, then, to accept the notion
that the being of light whom some have said found
humor in their sin could be the Jesus of the Bible. The
only beings who would mock sin and the biblical
picture of eternal punishment and judgment at the
hands of a holy God would be that crafty old liar,
Satan, or his servants.

The Bible teaches from Genesis to Revelation that
no person can meet God's standard of righteousness,
which is perfection, necessary to gain eternal life.
There is nothing that a person himself can do, learn or
develop which will result in his perfection so that he
can merit God's acceptance. For God is absolutely
holy and cannot tolerate sin in any form; sin is totally
alien to his very nature and character. Yet God is also
totally loving. He therefore provided a way for men
and women to be saved from the inevitable consequences of their sin through the atonement of a perfect sacrifice, God incarnate, Jesus the Christ. "For by
grace you have been saved through faith; and that not

of yourselves, *it is* the gift of God; not as a result of works, that no one should boast" (Eph. 2:8-9). There is, then, from a biblical perspective no acceptance of us by God apart from our acceptance of Jesus Christ's atonement through the shedding of his blood.

Moody seems confused at this point. He apparently mistakes Christ's or God's loving nature for a tolerance of sin. He cannot imagine his subjects who were not "rounders" but just "normal, nice" people being candidates for the "fiery pit." Clearly he is using his own human standard to judge the seriousness of sin in "normal, nice" people. God has said that we all deserve spiritual death or the "fiery pit," because of our sin. Whether we are "rounders" or "nice," we are all sinners before a holy God.

Moody's view is expressed again when he discusses what he feels should be the proper judgment on those who have committed terrible acts, such as the "perpetrators of the Nazi horrors." He feels that "hell" for such people would be to be confronted with all the torment and hurt which they caused. "In my wildest fantasies, I am totally unable to imagine a hell more horrible, more ultimately unbearable than this."[24] I submit that there is a hell much more unbearable than this. When they were alive such people were able to bear such confrontation. Why shouldn't they be able to do so in an afterlife?

Moody does not view evil as God does, nor does he accept the biblical teaching that we will not judge ourselves. Jesus Christ will judge us, and he will consign to hell those who have not accepted him as their Savior.

**Semantic Mysticism**    The being of light who confronted many of Moody's patients taught a doctrine completely at odds with the biblical doctrine of grace. He transmitted to them the notion that one's primary tasks in life are to learn how to love others and to acquire knowledge which will result in self-realization and self-development. The emphasis is changed from God to self—from what God has done for us to what we can do for ourselves. The being of light, then, seems to be teaching what we commonly know as secular humanism—that we can "save" ourselves, that we are our own gods and have no need of a Savior/Messiah. Since the central, crucial message— the gospel or "good news"—of the Bible is that God has provided such a Savior, we must choose between the message of this being of light and the message of the Scriptures. For if the being of light is to be believed, we would have to jettison all of the major doctrines of the Christian faith. A doctrine of self-realization or self-salvation implies a completely unbiblical view of the nature of God, the nature of man and the nature of salvation. The deity of Jesus would be superfluous. Even his status as a good, moral man and a great teacher would be doubtful. For, if the Jesus of the Bible gave one message while on earth and the being of light, a more advanced enlightened Jesus, has a contradictory message, then the Jesus of the Bible taught in error.

Likewise, it is clear that Moody's theology, shared in large measure by Kübler-Ross and Monroe, makes the biblical doctrine of grace irrelevant; it redefines the concept so that it becomes unrecognizable from a scriptural point of view. Furthermore, as my friend Russell Sorensen says, this theology emasculates the Law as given directly by God in the Old Testament, for according to Moody's being of light, our behavior in this life, right or wrong, moral or immoral, ethical or unethical, matters not one whit in terms of our eternal destiny or the determination of our state in life hereafter. To remove the doctrines concerning law and grace from Christianity is to destroy the faith, leaving only a shell of meaningless religious jargon. The biblical language as used by Moody is just a semantic mysticism, in Francis Schaeffer's term. It sounds like it means something genuinely Christian but, if it means anything at all, it means quite the opposite.

In summary, we are left with only two choices. Either we use the Bible to measure and judge experience—either our own or that of others—or we use experience to judge the Bible. The Bible itself clearly teaches that if we follow our experience we may readily be led into error with severe consequences. We are out of our depth, so to speak, and up against a fantastically intelligent, attractive and cunning enemy—Satan.

I believe, therefore, that those individuals who encountered a being of light who either told them a lie or let them return to normal life secure in a lie (that is, in a belief system that will not result in their reconciliation with God but rather in their eventual eternal separation from God) encountered not Christ or an angel of God, but rather the devil or one of his demonic agents. Of course it remains possible that some individuals do encounter an angel of God or possibly Jesus. But Moody does not suggest that his patients may be divided into two groups who encountered different beings of light—one "real" or godly and the other in disguise or a counterfeit. Nonetheless,

I would like to offer it as a possibility.

I do not suggest that a nonbeliever meeting an angel or Jesus under such circumstances would be harshly treated, or judged and condemned, because even though that person is clinically dead, he or she obviously has not yet crossed that final gulf, and therefore the time for such final judgment has not yet come. I do maintain that God is consistent and would not lead people into confusion. If they meet Christ or an angel-messenger of God, the message received would be totally consistent with God's revelation of himself in the Bible.

**Visions of Judgments**    I have personally encountered one person who had experiences on the edge of death which did not conform to the Moody and Kübler-Ross data in that some degree of judgment from an angel or from a being thought to be Jesus was evident. These accounts appear to be just as valid as any others. Therefore, Moody and Kübler-Ross have not been exposed to the full spectrum of near-death data or have chosen to ignore that which does not fit their biases.

A fellow Christian, Jerry Walker, related to me the following incident that occurred during surgery: "I have no idea how long I was without any sensation in that darkness. Then it was like I awoke and I knew it was real. In front of me, I watched my whole life pass by. Every thought, word, and every movement I had made in my life since the time I knew that Jesus was real. I was very young when I took Christ as my Savior. I saw things I had done which I had forgotten, but remembered as I watched them pass before me. This experience was, to say the least, unbelievable.

Every detail, right up to the present time. It all took place in what seemed like just a fraction of a second, and yet it was all very vivid.

"All the time I was watching my life go by, I felt the presence of some sort of power, but I didn't see it. Next, I was drawn into total darkness. Then I stopped. It felt like a big hollow room. It seemed to be a very large space, and totally dark. I could see nothing, but felt the presence of this power.

"I asked the power where I was and who he or it was. Communication was not by talking, but through a flow of energy. He answered that he was the Angel of Death. I believed him. The Angel went on to say that *my life was not what it should be* [emphasis mine], that he could take me on, but that I would be given a second chance, and that I was to go back. He promised me that I would not die in 1967.

"Next thing I remember, I was in the recovery room, back in my body. I was so taken in by this experience that I did not notice what kind of body I had, nor how much time had elapsed. It was so real—I believed it. ⚔

"Later in 1967, a car ran over my neck and shoulders. Still later that year, I was in a car wreck in which both cars were totalled, and in both accidents I came out almost completely unhurt. In neither accident was I at fault.

"I did not tell many people about my experience; I did not want to be considered crazy. But the encounter was very real to me, and I still believe that I was with the Angel of Death.

"I now serve Jesus with my whole heart and life in 1977. Praise God!"

Likewise, David Wheeler reports talking with a

man who had been involved in a serious automobile accident:

"I felt myself die. Suddenly I knew I was in heaven. Heaven was green in color. It was like a fresh, cool valley just after a Spring-time shower has passed over."

"What else did you see?"

"A cross."

"Are you religious?"

"Before the accident—No. After—yes!"

"Why the sudden transformation?"

"I saw Jesus on the cross. He didn't want me to stay there in heaven. Jesus kicked me out of heaven."

"I don't remember anything about the seven deaths that I had on the way to the hospital in the ambulance. I only remember that I died. I was surely in what I saw as heaven. And I did see Jesus, His blood, and a cross."[25]

These two accounts are very different from anything reported by Moody or Kübler-Ross and are more consistent with biblical teachings.

On the other hand, there are a number of near-death and out-of-the-body experiences which are even more unbiblical than those recounted by Moody. Wheeler relates the experience of Victor Solow who "experienced 'clinical' death for twenty-three minutes." Solow eventually says that he became a new "I": "I became an indestructible—pure spirit and pure energy. But I was not a separate entity anymore, for I had become a part of the universe." This experience seems to conform much more to a pantheistic version of reality than to anything recognizably Christian or generally theistic.[26]

**The Prince of This World** One might ask why God would permit demons or the devil to impersonate Jesus or one of his angels and thus deceive people during such an unusual and vulnerable time of crisis. These individuals have not yet left life in this earthly realm for good. They do return and recover from this state and thus were probably only on the edge of death but not really dead. Thus, according to the Bible they are still in the province of Satan. Jesus made that clear when he referred to the devil as the "prince" or "ruler" of this world (Jn. 12:31; 14:30). The Scriptures teach that the devil has leave to do his utmost to keep people in the darkness and bondage of their sin, unreconciled to their Creator for a period of time on this earth and in this existence until God calls a final halt to all of Satan's activities and he is cast into hell. The individuals in Moody's study were, therefore, still subject to the efforts of Satan to deceive them, and through the interpretations and conclusions drawn from their experiences the rest of us are subject to his efforts to turn us aside from the truth. What a great victory for Satan if he can use sincere people who believe they are transmitting a message from God about the life after this life to lull and lead many into the false belief that we only need to develop our ability to love and to gain more knowledge, that we need have no fear of a holy God judging or condemning us, that all of us will eventually end up with God in a heavenly existence, regardless of our acceptance or rejection of Jesus as Lord and Savior.

It is our responsibility as Christians to know the Scriptures well so that under the guidance of the Holy Spirit we can discern truth from error—or sort out a

mixture of truth and error—and so that we can discern between the real and the counterfeit, between
an angel of God and the devil disguised as an angel
of light.

# A Starting
# Point:
# Some
# Conclusions

# 6

When considering research, it is instructive to examine the biases of the investigators because these presuppositions and philosophies may well influence the interpretations placed upon the data and the conclusions finally drawn.

**No Fixed Doctrines: Moody**   Dr. Moody has indicated some of his beliefs and values in the introduction to *Life after Life*. He states:

    I have grown up having a "religion" not as a set of fixed doctrines, but rather as a concern with spiritual and religious doctrines, teachings, and questions. I believe that all the great religions of man have many truths to tell us, and I believe that no one of us has all the answers to the deep and

fundamental truths with which religion deals.[1]
Thus, Moody does not accept the Bible as infallible
and inerrant. He would undoubtedly find many of
Jesus' references to himself as narrow if not bigoted,
such as the statement: "I am *the* way, and *the* truth,
and *the* life; no one comes to the Father, but through
Me" (Jn. 14:6, emphasis mine). Jesus also said:

> Enter by the narrow gate; for the gate is wide, and
> the way is broad that leads to destruction, and
> many are those who enter by it. For the gate is
> small, and the way is narrow that leads to life, and
> few are those who find it. Beware of the false
> prophets, who come to you in sheep's clothing, but
> inwardly are ravenous wolves. . . . Not every one
> who says to Me, "Lord, Lord," will enter the king-
> dom of heaven; but he who does the will of My
> Father who is in heaven. Many will say to Me on
> that day [of future judgment], "Lord, Lord, did we
> not prophesy in Your name, and in Your name cast
> out demons, and in Your name perform many
> miracles?" And then I will declare to them, "I
> never knew you; DEPART FROM ME YOU WHO PRAC-
> TICE LAWLESSNESS." (Mt. 7:13-15, 21-23)

Besides seeing no value in many religious teachings,
Jesus specifically excluded all those that varied from
his own as false. He made it quite clear that when the
end comes, many "religious" people will be sepa-
rated from God forever.

Moody obviously has a different world view or set
of assumptions from those of Jesus. Moody does not
seem to accept any absolutes or authority from which
we can derive truth. Thus, he is open to any interpretation which he or others may wish to place upon his
patients' data or experiences. He is free to accept any

conclusion, even though that conclusion is a direct contradiction to what is taught in the Scriptures. It follows logically that he is also without any method whatsoever of distinguishing between truth and error because he has no yardstick with which to measure matters in the spiritual realm. If one takes the position that absolute truth and error do not exist (or if it exists we cannot know it) and all we really have are experiences which cannot be evaluated or judged by such criteria, then research itself is pointless because no conclusions can be drawn.

Moody's prior assumptions lead him in his discussion of parallel experiences to examine the Bible, particularly regarding Paul's conversion experience. However, he also examines Plato's dialogues, The Tibetan Book of the Dead and the writings of Emanuel Swedenborg (an occultic medium and Christian heretic) as though these writings were on a par with the Bible and equally authoritative. It is little wonder, then that Moody's conclusions, although not stated in a dogmatic fashion in view of his concept of openness, range far afield from biblical teachings.

In his latest book, Moody expresses concern that some "conservative" ministers have suggested "that near-death experiences are directed by satanic forces or evil demons."[2] He responds that some ministers have assured him that visions "must be consistent with what is stated in The Bible and have shared with me their feeling that this criterion is satisfied in this case."[3] I and others, however, would sharply differ with such reassurances for reasons previously discussed. Moody further states that although he is unsettled by the implication that he is "in league with the devil," he has been relieved to find that even a fundamentalist minister was accused of being a helper of Satan. He closes his discussion of this type of criticism in this way: "I dare say I must content myself with the reflection that in this huge, diverse world there will always be those who impugn one's motivation. I can but hope that, in the respects in which I am wrong, someone will come along to help lead me back to the correct path."[4]

Dr. Moody, in my opinion, has failed to confront the issue of satanic deception with respect to either his subjects' or his own interpretations of data. The question is not just one of Dr. Moody's motivation, although the motivation of any investigator in this field is certainly a valid subject for scrutiny, and the question is not whether he can find "men of the cloth" who will support him. The question is whether he has been deceived and is passing this deception along to his readers. This question can only be answered by reference to the Bible. If Dr. Moody is sincere in desiring guidance to truth, he (and anyone else of like mind) needs to begin first by totally submitting himself to Jesus Christ as Savior and Lord and to the complete authority of the Scriptures as the inerrant Word of God. Without being willing to submit to the Source of Truth, no one finds his way through such a quagmire of conflicting ideas.

**The Witness of the Spirits: Kübler-Ross**   It is somewhat more difficult to discern the presuppositions that undergird the work of Kübler-Ross since we must rely on somewhat sketchy information. Interviewers have apparently not asked about her own approach to the Bible. We know that she readily accepts the veracity of her spirit guides Salem, Anka and Willie;

and we know that she is constructing experiments in communication with the dead. So we can conclude that she is not concerned to wrestle with the biblical warning about necromancy. She simply places her faith in the evidence which she feels is coming from "the other side."

One problem with assuming that evidence from such spirit sources and mediumistic practices is veridical is that it is so various. If she does not know already, it would take very little time for her to learn that there are many conflicting reports of what happens on the other side. Among those who claim to have been there and back, some assume a theistic world where an infinite-personal God graciously welcomes his people as they pass from this life to the next. Some become one with something quite impersonal. Some depict a world where each person who dies becomes practically a god. Some experience hell, complete with fire and "lavalike, boiling mud."[5] Others like A. Alvarez in *The Savage God* come back totally disillusioned, having experienced nothing but "oblivion":

> I thought death would be like that: a synoptic vision of life, crisis by crisis, all suddenly explained, justified, redeemed, a Last Judgment in the coils and circuits of the brain. Instead all I got was a hole in the head, a round zero, nothing. I'd been swindled.[6]

The witness of mediums is no less various. As Gordon R. Lewis says,

> Spirit-messages contradict each other on the nature of Jesus Christ and other things. The spirits allegedly giving the messages and their content are extremely difficult to confirm as leading re-

searchers in Society of Psychical Research have acknowledged.[7]

This comment is well documented by D. Scott Rogo's summary of the phenomena surrounding the activity of mediums.[8]

If our data is self-contradictory, if the reports vary greatly, as indeed they do, we can certainly draw few incontestable conclusions—surely not enough on which to stake our spiritual life. Dr. Kübler-Ross, however, apparently pays scant attention to the variations in the data. Perhaps when her new research is published, she will take proper account of this problem.

### Naive Naturalism to Occult Evangelism: Monroe

Robert Monroe's story concerns not only journeys out of the body but also the journey of one man from naive naturalism to occult evangelism. A warning is implicit in Monroe's journey. He did not begin by thinking about philosophy or theology but rather by simply "experiencing." However, his journey resulted in a changed world view, a changed philosophy of life. In the course of his experiences, Monroe became very "religious," but his theology is certainly not Christian by biblical standards. Christians who are not well grounded in the truths of the Bible, who do not know well the content of the Scriptures, are similarly susceptible. Monroe was introduced to a spiritual world he never dreamed existed. In his search for explanations he seems to have assumed that his experiences can be accepted at face value.

There is a direct relationship at this point between Monroe's thinking and that of Moody and Kübler-Ross. None of them appears to question seriously whether or not they are being, or could be, deceived by clever satanic forces. Rather, they seem simply to put their trust or faith in their own intellectual powers of analysis and in the pronouncements of "spirit guides." They evaluate the Bible by their own experiences or that of others, rather than use biblical criteria to judge or sort out experiences. All are fascinated by the occult.

In reading about their experiences and those of their patients, many, including myself, find a real interest and curiosity stirred by the fantastic visions which they conjure up. Their writings are very seductive. Who does not dream of escaping the confines of the physical body and flying free of all inhibitions? We must, however, be careful not to let our fascination lead us into satanic deception.

Watchman Nee has suggested that Adam had powers which he lost as a result of the Fall.[9] Nee proposes that these abilities may correspond to what we think of as psychic powers. Nee's contention is that we are not legitimately permitted to use this "latent power of the soul," but rather we are to be totally dependent upon the power of the Holy Spirit in our lives.[10] Albrecht and Alexander have pointed out that

> from a biblical perspective, it would seem logical that the 90% of mental potential that lies fallow and unused can be traced to the fall of man and the resultant curse. Scripture suggests that our spiritual powers and perceptions were severely restricted. Yet, we are made in the image of God just as Adam and Eve were, even if that image has been somewhat corroded. It is fair to assume that those latent spiritual/intellectual capabilities (some may

call them "psychic" powers) can be aroused by certain stimuli—a brush with death, for example. Because these latent powers are aroused in the wrong context (i.e., in our fallen moral state, apart from God), the experiences or insights generated may be garbled, conflicting or incomplete, the last three adjectives accurately describing many of Moody's and Kübler-Ross's findings.[11]

**The Big Plum** In considering the biases of the investigators, it should also be noted that both Moody and Kübler-Ross are aware of what their work will lead to: "To solve the mystery of death, and to solve it with a note of optimism and an air of scientific certitude, puts them at least one notch above history's greatest kings, philosophers and prophets.... Both Moody and Kübler-Ross realize that this is indeed the big plum; to whomever dispels the mystery and fear of death, the reward is the mastery of life and the power and glory that go in hand with it."[12] Monroe has clearly indicated in his summary what might be considered an arrogant or condescending attitude toward biblical Christianity, and he has presented some imaginative thinking about the power which may accrue to those who can skillfully maneuver while out of the body. Imagine assassinating or sparing the lives of world leaders!

Dr. Moody and Dr. Kübler-Ross certainly seem to be sincere and compassionate individuals who want to help not only people who are in the process of dying but all the rest of us who will eventually face death. Kübler-Ross has mentioned her hurt and disappointment at the "abuse, insults and humiliation" that she has received from other physicians who consider her to be unscientific and from others who consider the whole topic to be taboo. She mentions one clergyman who complained that she was selling "cheap grace." One physician has told patients wishing to secure Dr. Kübler-Ross's counsel that she is "very sick."[13]

We must be careful, however, to attack what is false and deceptive rather than to attack personalities. As Christians, our real and final enemy is Satan rather than those, like these investigators, who promote a world view markedly at variance with what God has revealed. They, even with their good intentions, become pawns in an age-old game of deceit designed to lead astray not only those who have direct experiences with the devil in disguise but also those of us to whom those experiences are reported.

**Watchman, What of the Night?**      In my opinion, we will see an increasing drift toward a world religion which will be occult in nature. Such a religion will contain elements of Christianity, Judaism and perhaps Islam but will have as its base Eastern mysticism. As Christians find themselves an increasingly smaller minority, they will experience greater and greater pressure to become less "narrow minded" and "bigoted" and to become more open to this more "sophisticated" faith which, we will be told, is the apex of all previous religious systems. I believe that this occult world faith will appear to have validity because it will be accompanied by startling supernatural "signs and wonders" (Mk. 13:22). It will be hard, even for Christians, not to become part of such a system or at least to seek accommodation with it.

We must, therefore, hold fast to our standard by

which we are able to distinguish truth from error
and resist any attempt to dilute its authority. We
must, then, evaluate in the light of Scripture all such
research whether or not it is termed "scientific." We
must not simply discard all the data gathered by such
studies and bury ourselves intellectually in the sand
but rather take a serious look at all interpretations
placed upon such data. If the conclusions drawn are
contrary to the teachings of the Bible or lead people
away from finding a true relationship with God, we
must reject these conclusions. We must lead those
who would otherwise be deceived back to the clear
and certain sound of the Word of God.

# Notes

**Chapter 1**
[1]C. Stephen Board, "Light at the End of the Tunnel," *Eternity* (July 1977). p. 16.

**Chapter 2**
[1]Raymond A. Moody, Jr., *Life after Life* (New York: Bantam, 1976), p. 16. See also his further definitions of the terms *near-death experience* and *near-death encounter* in *Reflections on Life after Life* (New York: Bantam/Mockingbird, 1977), pp. 124-26.

[2]Ibid., pp. 25-26.

[3]William Standish Reed, *Surgery of the Soul* (Old Tappan: Fleming Revell, 1969), p. 83.

[4]Moody, *Life*, p. 32.

[5]Ibid., p. 42.

[6]Ibid., p. 43.

[7]Ibid., p. 54.

[8]Ibid., p. 55.

[9]Ibid., p. 59.

[10]Ibid., p. 60.

[11]Ibid., pp. 60-61.

[12]Ibid., p. 65.

[13]Ibid., p. 77.

[14]Ibid., p. 79.

[15]Ibid., p. 81.

[16]Ibid., p. 89.

[17]Ibid., p. 93.

[18]Ibid., p. 95.

[19]Ibid., p. 97.

[20]Moody, *Reflections*, p. 15.

[21]Ibid., p. 36.

[22]Ibid., p. 37.

[23]Ibid., p. 32.

[24]Moody, *Life*, pp. 98-101.

[25]Moody, *Reflections*, pp. 9-10.

[26]Ibid., p. 18.

[27]Moody, *Life*, p. 128.

[28]Ibid., pp. 181-82.

[29]Ibid., p. ix.

**Chapter 3**
[1]Elisabeth Kübler-Ross, *On Death and Dying* (New York: Macmillan, 1969); *Questions and Answers on Death and Dying* (New York: Macmillan, 1974).

[2]Ann Nietzke, "The Miracle of Kübler-Ross," *Human Behavior* (September 1977).

[3]Ibid., p. 21.

[4]Linda Witt, "Yes, There Is Life after Death," *Oui* (March 1977), p. 43.

[5]Lennie Kronisch, "Elisabeth Kübler-Ross: Messenger of Love," *Yoga Journal* (November-December 1976), p. 18.

[6]Witt, p. 44.

[7]Ibid., pp. 44, 131.

[8]Ibid., p. 134.

[9]Nietzke, p. 22.

[10]Ibid.

[11]Ibid., p. 24. Nietzke spells the name *Shantih Nilaya,* but this is surely in error since Kübler-Ross has founded a "healing and growth center" in the hills near Lake Wohlford in San Diego County, and she has called this center Shanti Nilaya; she envisions it as a branch of her planned Salem University which will promote the healing arts.

[12]Ibid., p. 23.

[13]Ibid., p. 24.

[14]Ibid.

[15]Ibid.

[16]Ibid., p. 25.

[17]Ibid.

[18]Ibid.

[19]Ibid.

[20]Kronisch, p. 20.

[21]Witt, pp. 131, 134.

**Chapter 4**

[1]Robert A. Monroe, *Journeys Out of the Body* (Garden City: Anchor, 1971), p. 33.

[2]Ibid., p. 20.

[3]Ibid., p. 28.

[4]Ibid.

[5]Ibid., p. 34.

[6]Ibid., p. 39. See also Phillip Swihart, *Reincarnation, Edgar Cayce and the Bible* Downers Grove: InterVarsity Press, 1975).

[7]Monroe, p. 116.

[8]Ibid., pp. 122-23.

[9]Ibid., p. 124.

[10]Ibid., p. 91.

[11]Ibid., p. 262.

[12]Ibid.

[13]Ibid., p. 266.

[14]Ibid.

[15]Ibid.

[16]Ibid., p. 267.

[17]Quoted in Mark Albrecht and Brooks Alexander, "Thanatology: Death and Dying," *Journal of the Spiritual Counterfeits Project* (April 1, 1977), p. 7.

[18]Ibid., p. 8.

[19]Ibid.

[20]Ibid., p. 8.

[21]Ibid., p. 6.

**Chapter 5**

[1]Moody, *Life,* p. 152. One reason for suggesting that the near-death experiences may in fact take place while the brain is still functioning and the body still very much alive is that similar experiences have occurred to people who were not near death. If the OOBE can be triggered in a perfectly alive person, is it not possible that the near-death OOBE is triggered in an equally "alive" person?

[2]Ibid., p. 148.

[3]John Weldon and Zola Levitt, *Is There Life after Death?* (Irvine: Harvest

House, 1977), p. 37.

[4]Moody, *Life*, p. 150; Weldon and Levitt, p. 35. See also the extended but lucid discussion of the definitions of death in Lyall Watson, *The Romeo Error* (New York: Dell, 1976), pp. 19-84.

[5]Ralph Wilkerson in *Beyond and Back* includes a number of other cases: the dead Moabite (2Kings 13:20-21), Jonah (Jon. 1:1—2:10), Jairus' daughter (Mk. 5:22-43). But it is doubtful that any of these people were really dead. In the cases I mention in the text the Scripture clearly indicates death had occurred. Second, Wilkerson has confused resuscitation of corpses with "resurrection." He includes in his list of "resurrections" the saints who rose from their tombs after the crucifixion (Mt. 27:50-53), Jesus' appearance to the apostle Paul in Acts 9:5 and the description of the resurrection to come in 1 Thessalonians 4:16-17. In fact, Lazarus and all the other resuscitated individuals died after their resuscitations and now await the resurrection in the last days. Jesus, on the other hand, has already been resurrected. His resurrection body is not a resuscitated corpse but a transformed body, coterminus with the one which went into the grave—after all, the grave was empty—but different in character from that of Lazarus' body. For Lazarus died again, but Jesus will never die again. See Ralph Wilkerson, *Beyond and Back: Those Who Died and Lived to Tell It* (Anaheim: Melodyland Productions, 1977), pp. 159-79.

[6]Moody, *Life*, p. 151.

[7]Witt, p. 134; and Monroe, pp. 173-78.

[8]G. S. Hendry comments on Ecclesiastes 12:6 as follows: "The figures of the *golden bowl* broken would seem to refer to the dissolution of soul and body. The life of a man is likened first to a golden bowl (containing oil for a lamp) suspended by a silver cord, then to a *pitcher* with which water is drawn from a well. The lamp and the pitcher were both familiar symbols of life in antiquity." (*The New Bible Commentary: Revised* [London: InterVarsity Press, 1970], p. 577.)

[9]Archie Matson also illustrates such a denegration of the body in his syncretistic book *Afterlife: Reports from the Threshold of Death* (New York: Harper and Row, 1975), pp. 127-31.

[10]Albrecht and Alexander, p. 9.

[11]David R. Wheeler, *Journey to the Other Side* (New York: Ace, 1977), p. 116.

[12]Ibid., p. 119.

[13]Ibid., pp. 122-23.

[14]Jack W. Provonsha, "Life after Life?" *The Ministry* (July 1977), p. 22.

[15]Monroe, pp. 138-39.

[16]Wilkerson, p. 19.

[17]See Board, p. 5.

[18]Ibid., p. 12.

[19]Albrecht and Alexander, p. 10.

[20]See Phillip J. Swihart, *How to Live with Your Feelings* (Downers Grove: InterVarsity Press, 1976), pp. 51-58.

[21]Moody, *Life*, p. 97.

[22]Ibid., p. 98.

[23]Ibid.

[24]Moody, *Reflections*, p. 39.

[25]Wheeler, pp. 65-66.

[26]Ibid., p. 13.
**Chapter 6**
[1]Moody, *Life*, p. 4.
[2]Moody, *Reflections*, p. 59.
[3]Ibid.
[4]Ibid., p. 60.
[5]Wheeler, p. 39.
[6]A. Alvarez, *The Savage God: A Study of Suicide* (London: Weidenfeld and Nicolson, 1971), pp. 235-36.
[7]Gordon R. Lewis, "Criteria for the Discerning of Spirits," in *Demon Possession: A Medical, Historical, Anthropological and Theological Symposium*, ed. John Warwick Montgomery (Minneapolis: Bethany Fellowship, 1976), pp. 352-53.
[8]D. Scott Rogo, *Man Does Survive Death: The Welcoming Silence* (Secaucus, NJ: Citadel, 1977; first published 1973), pp. 95-131.
[9]Watchman Nee, *The Latent Power of the Soul* (New York: Christian Fellowship Publishers, 1972).
[10]Swihart, *Reincarnation*, p. 49.
[11]Albrecht and Alexander, p. 9.
[12]Ibid., p. 8.
[13]Nietzke, p. 27.

## Annotated Bibliography

The following bibliography is designed to help readers who wish to pursue the topic of life after life in more depth. The specific materials singled out for comment include not only the major sources for the present volume but other works often more wide-ranging in content as well as in perspective. The annotations, sometimes both critical and descriptive, are designed to serve as a guide through the quagmire of conflicting evidence and interpretation. No attempt has been made to achieve completeness. Readers will find those books with bibliographies, notably Watson's *The Romeo Error* and Weldon and Levitt's *Is There Life after Death?*, especially useful.

---

Albrecht, Mark and Brooks Alexander. "Thanatology: Death and Dying," *Journal of the Spiritual Counterfeits Project*, April 1977, pp. 5-11.
This discerning Christian critique sets the subject of thanatology in its historical and cultural context, points out the links between spiritism and technology, and analyzes the nature of OOBEs, concluding that, "in view of the necromantic connections of the leading thanatologists, the obvious biblical inference must be drawn—that there is a potential of outright demonic collusion and otherworldly manip-

ulations of mental states."

---

Board, C. Stephen. "Light at the End of the Tunnel," *Eternity*, July 1977, pp. 13-17, 30-33.

This inquiry by a noted Christian journalist not only summarizes the main features of the life-after-life controversy but includes the results of some investigative reporting, especially drawing on Christian physicians and theologians who have not yet published their views. A helpful, basic critique.

---

Coombs, Peter. *Life after Death*. Downers Grove: InterVarsity Press, 1978.

In a straightforward and simple manner Peter Coombs explains the Bible's teaching about the afterlife. This short (32-page) booklet is a good piece to pass on to friends who have been impressed with the sensational stories and with the nonbiblical conclusions of Moody, Kübler-Ross and others. For a more extensive treatment, see Zodhiates, *Life after Death?*, listed below (p. 96).

---

Harlow, S. Ralph. *A Life after Death*. New York: Manor Books, 1968.

Despite his claim that he is "not a spiritualist" but a Christian with interest in psychic research, Harlow not only surveys the scientific aspects of psychic phenomena but details for us his own contact with mediums and other manifestations of the occult world. From a liberal Christian background (he studied under Harry Emerson Fosdick at Union Theological Seminary), Harlow came to realize that there is much reality in the psychic world. He found that when he read the Bible from this perspective, the life of Jesus and the historic events in the Gospels took on "significance and meaning" (p. 60). One chapter is devoted to a psychic interpretation of the New Testament, commenting on such events as the visions of Peter, the transfiguration and the resurrection of Christ. The disciples, he says, were wrong about the resurrection. Jesus' body was not raised from the grave and transformed. Rather, "it was His astral body that survived the death of the physical body" (p. 169). This book, like Archie Matson's *Afterlife* (see below), seems to be a disingenuous attempt to view Christianity totally in terms of occult philosophy; the philosophy interprets the Bible rather than the Bible, philosophy.

---

Lewis, Gordon R. "Criteria for the Discerning of Spirits" *Demon Possession: A Medical, Historical, Anthropological and Theological Symposium.* Ed. John Warwick Montgomery. Minneapolis: Bethany Fellowship, 1976, pp. 346-63.

Theologian Lewis gives in brief form a useful set of criteria for discerning whether demons are involved in any specific, seemingly psychic activity. He argues that, rather than deciding beforehand what God might or might not wish to do through spiritual means (for example, miraculous healings), we keep our minds open and our attentions alert. Since, he argues, God cannot lie, the good spirits in following him will maintain accuracy and consistency. The message brought by good spirits will "empirically fit"; there will be no logical contradiction in what they say; and the message will have an existential viability in the sense that we will be able to live within its terms. He argues that biblical revelation fits these criteria well but that, "in contrast, the spiritualists' hypothesis of communication with spirits of the dead in an evolutionary universe with an impersonal, immanent God fails to meet the criteria of truth. Spirit-messages contradict each other on the nature of Jesus Christ and other things. The spirits allegedly giving the messages and their content are extremely difficult to confirm as leading researchers of the society of psychical research have acknowledged" (pp. 352-53). Good spirits can be detected by their moral character: their chief end is "God's pleasure"; their supreme authority is "God's Word"; and their pre-eminent message is "God's gospel."

---

Matson, Archie. *Afterlife: Reports from the Threshold of Death.* New York: Harper & Row, 1975.

In this book, originally published under the title *The Waiting World* (1975) Archie Matson, a liberal Protestant minister, presents a mixture of Christianity and the occult. While many of his ideas have some basis in the Scripture, Matson's authority lies elsewhere: "Mediumship spells out in much greater detail and perhaps accuracy a picture of the waiting world to which our earlier chapters on the Bible, science, deathbed scenes, apparitions and Lazarus experiences can only point in a partial and shadowy way.... Mediumship is the crown which gives confirmation and clarity to all the rest" (p. 74). Matson constructs a geography of the afterlife, arguing that there are a number of different places (or states), none of which really parallels the biblical heaven or hell. Moreover, any kind of hell into which those who die are drawn will only be short-lived: "Hell is a temporary state, lasting until we have had enough and are ready to change" (p. 107). In his chapter on the Bible as "shackle or spur," Matson finds a number of contradictions (none of these are really contradictions if one takes the time to investigate), and he finds two mutually exclusive views of what life after death is like according to the Bible. A major problem in his understanding of the New Testament is his refusal to consider the seriousness with which the Old and New Testament writers considered the value of the body. He projects his own more Platonic view onto the New Testament passages and finds some of these in conflict with others. Matson's book deserves critical study, if only to show what happens when an attempt is made to read the Old and New Testaments in light of occult presuppositions.

---

Monroe, Robert A. *Journeys Out of the Body*. Garden City: Anchor, 1971.

Monroe tells the story of how he came accidentally to have out-of-the-body experiences and then began to study their nature and character. This book is summarized and critiqued in chapters four, five and six of this work.

---

Moody, Raymond A., Jr. *Life after Life*. New York: Bantam, 1976.

First published in November 1975 by Mockingbird, this book quickly rose to best-seller status and continued for many months on the charts. It is widely read on university campuses as well as by the general public. While by no means the first book of its kind, its success has stimulated a flood of similar books and a sequel as well. This book is summarized in chapter two and critiqued in chapters five and six.

---

Moody, Raymond A., Jr. *Reflections on Life after Life.* New York: Bantam/Mockingbird, 1977.

This sequel to his highly successful predecessor presents four additional common elements of near-death experiences. Moody, who has always appeared to be cautious not to claim too much for his work, is even more cautious in this book. Of peculiar interest are Moody's comments on how Christians have reacted to *Life after Life*—some telling him that his work confirms the things they believe for other reasons, others commenting that they believe that his work is consistent with what is stated in the Bible, and still others warning that the near-death experiences are demonic. Moody also fills in a gap in the earlier book by presenting some of the parallel accounts from well-known figures, such as C. G. Jung, Ernest Hemingway and Leo Tolstoy. He closes with a superficial discussion of methodological considerations involved with doing life-after-life research. A bibliography is appended.

---

Myers, John. *Voices from the Edge of Eternity.* Old Tappan: Spire, 1976.

This is a totally uncritical compilation of death-bed stories and near-death experiences gleaned from contemporary sources and several nineteenth-century works: D. P. Kidder, *Dying Hours* (1848), A. H. Gottschall, *Dying Words* (1888) and S. B. Shaw, *Dying Testimonies* (1898). The nearly two hundred fifty separate accounts concern such historical figures as Ethan Allen, Anne Boleyn, John Calvin, Martin Luther, Dwight L. Moody and Joan of Arc. Compiled from the standpoint of one who wishes to demonstrate the truth of Scripture, these stories focus on the positive aspects of those who died expressing faith in God and the negative character of the experiences of those like the "infidel" Voltaire whose death "was a scene of horror that lies beyond all exaggeration" (p. 23). Of little evidential value.

---

Nietzke, Ann. "The Miracle of Kübler-Ross," *Human Behavior*, September 1977, pp. 18-27.
   This article profiles Dr. Kübler-Ross on the basis of a long, detailed interview. Chapter three above is largely based on this account.

---

Rogo, D. Scott. *Man Does Survive Death: The Welcoming Silence*. Secaucus, N.J.: The Citadel Press, 1977.
   First published in 1973 as *The Welcoming Silence*, this book is a basic survey of "the major types of evidence that psychical research offers which indicate that the human personality survives death" (p. 9). The evidence he surveys includes OOBEs, experiments conducted as people are in the process of dying, deathbed visions and messages from the other side through mediumship. The problematic nature of messages that come through mediums is detailed by a survey of a number of famous mediums. In spite of this, Rogo places considerable confidence in many of their accounts. Bibliography included.

---

Watson, Lyall. *The Romeo Error: A Meditation on Life and Death*. New York: Dell, 1976.
   This wide-ranging survey by a trained biologist is a well-documented summary of much standard scientific work as well as psychic research relating to the nature of death, dying, the relationship between body

and mind, the question of survival without the body, possession by other spirits and miracles of healing. The book recounts along the way how the author has moved from the perspective of naturalism to a high respect for psychic research and the possibility of spiritual forces beyond: "I am driven to the conclusion that there is form in the void. You may call it God if you like" (p. 221). Much better written than most books on this subject, Watson's book would be a good place to start in understanding the life-after-life issues from the standpoint of a naturalist turned apologist for the world of psychic phenomena. The bibliography and index are extensive and helpful. Especially useful is the long and detailed chapter on the various definitions of death.

---

Weldon, John and Zola Levitt. *Is There Life after Death?* Irvine: Harvest House, 1977.

This is one of the better books from a Christian standpoint. In many ways it parallels the perspective of the present book, occasionally taking up subjects only tangentially touched on here, for example, the biblical teaching on the afterlife. It is a book well worth putting in the hands of those influenced by Moody, Kübler-Ross and Monroe.

---

Wheeler, David. R. *Journey to the Other Side.* New York: Ace, 1977.

This is a popular and in some ways slapdash account of a host of issues surrounding near-death experiences. In general, he aligns himself with Moody, Kübler-Ross and Monroe, though he does document a greater range of OOBEs and near-death experiences. His basic optimism is unguarded: "The Other Side awaits all of us. Some have visited for a short time and have returned to tell us of the joys and peacefulness in the hereafter. Some are now practicing ways to go and see the next world. The Other Side does exist and it will be everything that we want it to be" (p. 49).

White, Stewart Edward. *The Unobstructed Universe.* New York: E. P. Dutton, 1940.

White, who makes no pretense of being Christian, treats the afterlife totally within the framework of occult philosophy. He claims to get his view of reality from contact with the spirit world through his wife, Betty, and a friend, Joan, also a psychic. For a number of years "communication with the Invisibles, disincarnate earth-entities, had been of daily occurrence" in the author's home (p. 16). White and his wife wrote four books together, and then his wife, Betty, died. From the other side she contacted White through Joan. The book itself constructs an occult metaphysic ranging from astrophysics to consciousness. It and other books by White are occasionally referred to in life-after-death materials written from an occult perspective.

Wilkerson, Ralph. *Beyond and Back: Those Who Died and Lived to Tell It.* Anaheim: Melodyland Productions, 1977.

Wilkerson claims to answer such questions as: Do those in heaven see what is going on down here? Will I know my loved ones there? Will a baby remain an infant in heaven? Where exactly is heaven in the universe? Basing almost everything he has to say on the experience of a few Christians whom he believes have died and gone at least part way to heaven—some of

**96**

them all the way there—Wilkerson writes a book which majors in sensationalism. His discussion ranges widely from accounts of healing (which he calls a "minor resurrection") to accounts of resurrections in Indonesia, discussions of whether Karen Quinlan should be allowed to die and a curious tale of how Howard Hughes almost put Melodyland in his will. The questionable theological thinking is reflected in the summary of the biblical data on death, resuscitation and resurrection (see my footnote 5 on page 85 of the present volume). While Wilkerson is aware of the early work of Dr. Kübler-Ross, he seems unaware of her most recent occult connections. And, while he recognizes that "a fine line of distinction exists between the occult and the spiritual," his guidelines for discernment are sketchy (see pp. 59-60 and 220-22). The result is a book which could serve to encourage naive Christians to experiment with OOBEs.

---

Zodhiates, Spiros. *Life after Death?* Richfield, N.J.: AMG Publishers, 1977.

Bible scholar Zodhiates conducts a guided tour through the biblical data answering a host of questions about the afterlife: What is death? Where do the departed spirits go? Where is Sheol? What is Hades? Will the wicked suffer eternally? This sane and detailed analysis makes a good antidote for those who have been influenced to see the Bible through occult-colored glasses. For a brief treatment, see Coombs, *Life after Death*, listed above (p. 88).